YOUR PERSONAL
HOROSCOPE
2019

♓

PISCES

YOUR PERSONAL HOROSCOPE 2019

PISCES

20th February–20th March

igloobooks

Published in 2018
by Igloo Books Ltd
Cottage Farm
Sywell
NN6 0BJ
www.igloobooks.com

FIR003 0718
2 4 6 8 10 9 7 5 3 1
ISBN: 978-1-78810-537-8

This is an abridged version of material originally published
in Old Moore's Horoscope and Astral Diary.

Cover designed by Nicholas Gage
Edited by Bobby Newlyn-Jones

Printed and manufactured in China

CONTENTS

INTRODUCTION

Your personal horoscopes have been specifically created to allow you to get the most from astrological patterns and the way they have a bearing on not only your zodiac sign, but nuances within it. Using the diary section of the book you can read about the influences and possibilities of each and every day of the year. It will be possible for you to see when you are likely to be cheerful and happy or those times when your nature is in retreat and you will be more circumspect. The diary will help to give you a feel for the specific 'cycles' of astrology and the way they can subtly change your day-to-day life. For example, when you see the sign ☿, this means that the planet Mercury is retrograde at that time. Retrograde means it appears to be running backwards through the zodiac. Such a happening has a significant effect on communication skills, but this is only one small aspect of how the personal horoscope can help you.

With your personal horoscope the story doesn't end with the diary pages. It includes simple ways for you to work out the zodiac sign the Moon occupied at the time of your birth, and what this means for your personality. In addition, if you know the time of day you were born, it is possible to discover your Ascendant, yet another important guide to your personal make-up and potential.

Many readers are interested in relationships and in knowing how well they get on with people of other astrological signs. You might also be interested in the way you appear to very different sorts of individuals. If you are such a person, the section on Venus will be of particular interest. Despite the rapidly changing position of this planet, you can work out your Venus sign, and learn what bearing it will have on your life.

Using your personal horoscope you can travel on one of the most fascinating and rewarding journeys that anyone can take – the journey to a better realisation of self.

THE ESSENCE OF PISCES

Exploring the Personality of Pisces the Fishes

(20TH FEBRUARY – 20TH MARCH)

What's in a sign?

Pisceans are fascinating people – everyone you come across is likely to admit that fact. By nature you are kind, loving, trustful and inclined to work very hard on behalf of the people you love – and perhaps even those you don't like very much. Your nature is sympathetic and you will do anything you can to improve the lot of those you consider to be worse off than yourself. There is a very forgiving side to your temperament and also a strong artistic flair that can find an outlet in any one of a dozen different ways.

It's true you are difficult to know, and there is a very important reason for this. Your nature goes deep, so deep in fact that someone would have to live with you for a lifetime to plumb even a part of its fathomless depths. What the world sees is only ever a small part of the total magic of this most compulsive and fascinating zodiac sign. Much of your latent power and natural magic is constantly kept bottled up, because it is never your desire to manipulate those around you. Rather, you tend to wait in the shadows until opportunities to come into your own present themselves.

In love you are ardent and sincere, though sometimes inclined to choose a partner too readily and too early. There is a dreamy quality to your nature that makes you incredibly easy to adore, but which can also cause difficulties if the practical necessities of life take a very definite second place.

The chances are that you love music and picturesque scenery, and you may also exhibit a definite fondness for animals. You prefer to live in the country rather than in the middle of a noisy and smelly town, and tend to keep a reasonably well-ordered household. Your family can easily become your life and you always need a focus for your energies. You are not at all good at feathering your own nest, unless you know that someone else is also going to benefit on the way. A little more selfishness probably would not go amiss on occasions because you are often far too willing to put yourself out wholesale for people who don't respect your sacrifices. Pisceans can be full of raging passions and are some of the most misunderstood people to be found anywhere within the great circle of the zodiac.

Pisces resources

It is the very essence of your zodiac sign that you are probably sitting there and saying to yourself 'Resources? I have no resources'. Of course you are wrong, though it has to be admitted that a glaring self-confidence isn't likely to be listed amongst them. You are, however, a very deep thinker, and this can turn out to be a great advantage and a useful tool when it comes to getting on in life. Because your natural intuition is so strong (some people would call you psychic), you are rarely fooled by the glib words of others. Your own natural tendency to tell the truth can be a distinct advantage and a great help to you when it comes to getting on in life from a practical and financial viewpoint.

Whilst many of the signs of the zodiac tend to respond to life in an impulsive way, you are more likely to weigh up the pros and cons of any given situation very carefully. This means that when you do take action you can achieve much more success – as well as saving a good deal of energy on the way. People tend to confide in you automatically, so you are definitely at an advantage when it comes to knowing what makes your family and friends tick. At work you can labour quietly and confidently, either on your own or in the company of others. Some people would assert that Pisceans are model employees because you really do not know how to give anything less than your best.

Never underestimate the power of your instincts. Under most circumstances you are aware of the possible outcome of any given situation and should react as your inner mind dictates. Following this course inevitably puts you ahead of the game and explains why so quiet a sign can promote so many winners in life. Not that you are particularly competitive. It's much more important for you to be part of a winning team than to be out there collecting the glory for yourself.

You are dependable, kind, loving and peerless in your defence of those you take to. All of these are incredible resources when used in the correct way. Perhaps most important of all is your ability to get others on your side. In this you cannot be matched.

Beneath the surface

Everyone instinctively knows that there is something very important going on beneath the surface of the Piscean mind, though working out exactly what it might be is a different kettle of fish altogether. The fact is that you are very secretive about yourself and tend to give very little away. There are occasions when this tendency can be a saving grace, but others where it is definitely a great disadvantage. What isn't hard to see is your natural sympathy and your desire to help those in trouble. There's no end gain here, it's simply the way you are. Your inspiration to do anything is rarely rooted in what your own prize is likely to be. In your soul you are poetical, deeply romantic and inextricably tied to the forces and cycles of the world that brought you to birth.

Despite your capacity for single-minded concentration in some matters, you are often subject to mental confusion. Rational considerations often take second place to intuitive foresight and even inspiration. Making leaps in logic isn't at all unusual for you and forms part of the way you judge the world and deal with it.

If you really want to get on in life, and to gain the most you can from your interactions with others, you need to be very truthful in your approach. Somehow or other that means finding out what is really going on in your mind and explaining it to those around you. This is never going to be an easy process, partly because of your naturally secretive ways. Actually some astrologers overplay the tendency of Pisces to keep its secrets. A great deal of the time you simply don't think you have anything to say that would interest others and you always lack confidence in your own judgements. This is a shame because you rarely proceed without thinking carefully and don't often make glaring mistakes.

Many Pisceans develop an ingrained tendency to believe themselves inadequate in some way. Once again this is something you should fight against. Knowing others better, and allowing them to get to know you, might cause you to feel less quirky or strange. Whether you realise it or not you have a natural magnetism that draws others towards you. Try to spend rather less time thinking – though without losing that Piscean ability to meditate which is central to your well-being. If you allow the fascinating world of the Piscean mind to be shared by the people you come to trust, you should become more understandable to people who really want to like you even more.

Making the best of yourself

It must be remembered that the zodiac sign of Pisces represents two Fishes, tethered by a cord but constantly trying to break away from each other. This says a great deal about the basic Piscean nature. The inward, contemplative side of your personality is often at odds with the more gregarious and chatty qualities you also possess. Learning about this duality of nature can go at least part of the way towards dealing with it.

Although you often exhibit a distinct lack of self-confidence in your dealings with the world at large, you are, at heart, quite adept, flexible and able to cope under almost any circumstance. All that is really required in order to have a positive influence on life and to be successful is for you to realise what you are capable of achieving. Alas this isn't quite as easy as it might appear, because the introspective depths of your nature make you think too much and cause you to avoid the very actions that would get you noticed more. This can be something of a dilemma for Pisces, though it is certainly not insurmountable.

Never be afraid to allow your sensitivity to show. It is one of your greatest assets and it is part of the reason why other people love you so much – far more, in fact, than you probably realise. Your natural warmth, grace and charm are certain to turn heads on those occasions when you can't avoid being watched. The creative qualities that you possess make it possible for you to manufacture harmonious surroundings, both for yourself and for your family, who are very important to you. At the same time you recognise the practical in life and don't mind getting your hands dirty, especially when it comes to helping someone else out of a mess.

One of the best ruses Pisceans can use in order to get over the innate shyness that often attends the sign is to put on an act. Pisceans are very good natural actors and can easily assume the role of another individual. So, in your dealings with the world at large, manufacture a more confident individual, though without leaving out all the wonderful things that make you what you are now. Play this part for all you are worth and you will then truly be making the best of yourself.

The impressions you give

There is absolutely no doubt that you are more popular, admired and even fancied than you could ever believe. Such is the natural modesty of your zodiac sign that you invariably fail to pick up on those little messages coming across from other people that say 'I think you are wonderful'. If we don't believe in ourselves it's difficult for us to accept that others think we are worth their consideration. Failing to realise your worth to the world at large is likely to be your greatest fault and needs to be corrected.

In a way it doesn't matter, when seen from the perspective of others. What they observe is a warm-hearted individual. Your magnetic personality is always on display, whether you intend it to be or not, which is another reason why you tend to attract far more attention than you would sometimes elicit. Most Pisceans are quite sexy, another quality that is bound to come across to the people you meet, at least some of whom would be willing to jump through hoops if you were to command it.

In short, what you show, and what you think you are, could be two entirely different things. If you don't believe this to be the case you need to carry out a straw poll amongst some of the people you know. Ask them to write down all your qualities as they see them. The result will almost certainly surprise you and demonstrate that you are far more capable, and loveable, than you believe yourself to be. Armed with this knowledge you can walk forward in life with more confidence and feel as content inside as you appear to be when viewed by the world at large.

People rely heavily on you. That much at least you will have noticed in a day-to-day sense. They do so because they know how well you deal with almost any situation. Even in a crisis you show your true colours and that's part of the reason why so many Piscean people find themselves involved in the medical profession. You are viewed as being stronger than you believe yourself to be, which is why everyone tends to be so surprised when they discover that you are vulnerable and inclined to worry.

The way forward

You have a great deal to offer the world, even if you don't always appreciate how much. Although you are capable of being shy and introverted on occasions, you are equally likely to be friendly, chatty and very co-operative. You settle to just about any task, though you do possess a sense of freedom that makes it difficult for you to be cooped up in the same place for days and weeks at a stretch. You prefer the sort of tasks that allow your own natural proclivities to shine out, and you exhibit an instinctive creative tendency in almost anything you do.

Use your natural popularity to the full. People are always willing to put themselves out on your behalf, mainly because they know how generous you are and want to repay you for some previous favour. You should never be too proud to accept this sort of proffered help and must avoid running away with the idea that you are unequal to any reasonable task that you set yourself.

It's true that some of your thoughts are extremely deep and that you can get yourself into something of a brown study on occasions, which can be translated by the world around you as depression. However, you are far more stable than you probably believe yourself to be because Pisces is actually one of the toughest of the zodiac signs.

Because you are born of a Water sign it is likely that you would take great delight in living near the sea, or some other large body of water. This isn't essential to your well-being but it does feed your imagination. The vastness of nature in all its forms probably appeals to you in any case and most Pisceans love the natural world with its staggering diversity.

In love you are ardent and sincere, but you do need to make sure that you choose the right individual to suit you. Pisceans often settle for a protecting arm, but if this turns out to be stifling, trouble could follow. You would find it hard to live with anyone who didn't have at least a degree of your sensitivity, and you need a partner who will allow you to retain that sense of inner freedom that is so vital to your well-being.

Make the most of the many gifts and virtues that nature has bestowed upon you and don't be afraid to let people know what you really are. Actually establishing this in the first place isn't easy for you. Pisceans respond well to almost any form of meditation, which is not surprising because the sign of the Fishes is the most spiritually motivated zodiac sign of them all. When you know yourself fully you generate a personality that is an inspiration to everyone.

14

PISCES ON THE CUSP

Astrological profiles are altered for those people born at either the beginning or the end of a zodiac sign, or, more properly, on the cusps of a sign. In the case of Pisces this would be on the 20th of February and for two or three days after, and similarly at the end of the sign, probably from the 18th to the 20th of March.

The Aquarius Cusp – 20th February to 22nd February

This tends to be a generally happy combination of signs, even if some of the people you come into contact with find you rather difficult to understand from time to time. You are quite capable of cutting a dash, as any Aquarian would be, and yet at the same time you have the quiet and contemplative qualities more typified by Pisces. You tend to be seen as an immensely attractive person, even if you are the last one in the world to accept this fact. People find you to be friendly, very approachable and good company in almost any social or personal setting. It isn't hard for you to get on with others, though since you are not so naturally quiet as Pisces when taken alone, you are slightly more willing to speak your mind and to help out, though usually in a very diplomatic manner.

At work you are very capable and many people with this combination find themselves working on behalf of humanity as a whole. Thus work in social services, hospitals or charities really suits the unique combinations thrown up by this sign mixture. Management is right up your street, though there are times when your conception of popularity takes the foremost place in your mind. Occasionally this could take the edge off executive decisions. A careful attention to detail shows you in a position to get things done, even jobs that others shun. You don't really care for getting your hands dirty but will tackle almost any task if you know it to be necessary. Being basically self-sufficient, you also love the company of others, and it is this adaptability that is the hallmark of success to Aquarian-cusp Pisceans.

Few people actually know you as well as they think they do because the waters of your nature run quite deep. Your real task in life is to let the world know how you feel, something you fight shy of doing now and again. There are positive gains in your life, brought about as a result of your adaptable and pleasing nature. Aquarius present in the nature allows Pisces to act at its best.

The Aries Cusp – 18th March to 20th March

This is a Piscean with attitude and probably one of the most difficult zodiac sign combinations to be understood, not only by those people with whom you come into contact but clearly by yourself too. If there are any problems thrown up here they come from the fact that Pisces and Aries have such different ways of expressing themselves to the world at large. Aries is very upfront, dynamic and dominant, all factors that are simply diametrically opposed to the way Pisces thinks and behaves. So the real task in life is to find ways to combine the qualities of Pisces and Aries, in a way that suits the needs of both and without becoming totally confused with regard to your basic nature.

The problem is usually solved by a compartmentation of life. For example, many people with this combination will show the Aries qualities strongly at work, whilst dropping into the Piscean mode socially and at home. This may invariably be the case but there are bound to be times when the underlying motivations become mixed, which can confuse those with whom you come into contact.

Having said all of this you can be the least selfish and most successful individual when you are fighting for the rights of others. This is the zodiac combination of the true social reformer, the genuine politician and the committed pacifist. It seems paradoxical to suggest that someone could fight tenaciously for peace, but this is certainly true in your case. You have excellent executive skills and yet retain an ability to tell other people what they should be doing, in fairly strident terms, usually without upsetting anyone. There is a degree of genuine magic about you that makes you very attractive and there is likely to be more than one love affair in your life. A steadfast view of romance may not be naturally present within your basic nature but like so much else you can 'train' this quality into existence.

Personal success is likely, but it probably doesn't matter all that much in a material sense. The important thing to you is being needed by the world at large.

PISCES AND ITS ASCENDANTS

The nature of every individual on the planet is composed of the rich variety of zodiac signs and planetary positions that were present at the time of their birth. Your Sun sign, which in your case is Pisces, is one of the many factors when it comes to assessing the unique person you are. Probably the most important consideration, other than your Sun sign, is to establish the zodiac sign that was rising over the eastern horizon at the time that you were born. This is your Ascending or Rising sign. Most popular astrology fails to take account of the Ascendant, and yet its importance remains with you from the very moment of your birth, through every day of your life. The Ascendant is evident in the way you approach the world, and so, when meeting a person for the first time, it is this astrological influence that you are most likely to notice first. Our Ascending sign essentially represents what we appear to be, while the Sun sign is what we feel inside ourselves.

The Ascendant also has the potential for modifying our overall nature. For example, if you were born at a time of day when Pisces was passing over the eastern horizon (this would be around the time of dawn) then you would be classed as a double Pisces. As such, you would typify this zodiac sign, both internally and in your dealings with others. However, if your Ascendant sign turned out to be a Fire sign, such as Aries, there would be a profound alteration of nature, away from the expected qualities of Pisces.

One of the reasons why popular astrology often ignores the Ascendant is that it has always been rather difficult to establish. We have found a way to make this possible by devising an easy-to-use table, which you will find on page 157 of this book. Using this, you can establish your Ascendant sign at a glance. You will need to know your rough time of birth, then it is simply a case of following the instructions.

For those readers who have no idea of their time of birth it might be worth allowing a good friend, or perhaps your partner, to read through the section that follows this introduction. Someone who deals with you on a regular basis may easily discover your Ascending sign, even though you could have some difficulty establishing it for yourself. A good understanding of this component of your nature is essential if you want to be aware of that 'other person' who is responsible for the way you make contact with the world at large. Your Sun sign, Ascendant sign, and the other pointers in this book will, together, allow you a far better understanding of what makes you tick as an individual. Peeling back the different layers of your astrological make-up can be an enlightening experience, and the Ascendant may represent one of the most important layers of all.

Pisces with Pisces Ascendant

You are a kind and considerate person who would do almost anything to please the people around you. Creative and extremely perceptive, nobody knows the twists and turns of human nature better than you do, and you make it your business to serve humanity in any way you can. Not everyone understands what makes you tick, and part of the reason for this state of affairs is that you are often not really quite 'in' the world as much as the people you encounter in a day-to-day sense. At work you are generally cheerful, though you can be very quiet on occasions, but since you are consistent in this regard, you don't attract adverse attention or accusations of being moody, as some other variants of Pisces sometimes do. Confusion can beset you on occasions, especially when you are trying to reconcile your own opposing needs. There are certain moments of discontent to be encountered which so often come from trying to please others, even when to do so goes against your own instincts.

As age and experience add to your personal armoury you relax more with the world and find yourself constantly sought out for words of wisdom. The vast majority of people care for you deeply.

Pisces with Aries Ascendant

Although not an easy combination to deal with, the Pisces with an Aries Ascendant does bring something very special to the world in the way of natural understanding allied to practical assistance. It's true that you can sometimes be a dreamer, but there is nothing wrong with that as long as you have the ability to turn some of your wishes into reality, and this you are usually able to do, often for the sake of those around you. Conversation comes easily to you, though you also possess a slightly wistful and poetic side to your nature, which is attractive to the many people who call you a friend. A natural entertainer, you bring a sense of the comic to the often serious qualities of Aries, though without losing the determination that typifies the sign.

In relationships you are ardent, sincere and supportive, with a social conscience that sometimes finds you fighting the battles of the less privileged members of society. Family is important to you and this is a combination that invariably leads to parenthood. Away from the cut and thrust of everyday life you relax more fully, and think about matters more deeply than more typical Aries types might.

Pisces with Taurus Ascendant

You are clearly a very sensitive type of person and that sometimes makes it rather difficult for others to know how they might best approach you. Private and deep, you are nevertheless socially inclined on many occasions. However, because your nature is bottomless it is possible that some types would actually accuse you of being shallow. How can this come about? Well, it's simple really. The fact is that you rarely show anyone what is going on in the deepest recesses of your mind and so your responses can appear to be trite or even ill-considered. This is far from the truth, as those who are allowed into the 'inner sanctum' would readily admit. You are something of a sensualist, and relish staying in bed late and simply pleasing yourself for days on end. However, you have Taurean traits so you desire a tidy environment in which to live your usually long life.

You are able to deal with the routine aspects of life quite well and can be a capable worker once you are up and firing on all cylinders. It is very important that you maintain an interest in what you are doing, because the recesses of your dreamy mind can sometimes appear to be infinitely more attractive. Your imagination is second to none and this fact can often be turned to your advantage.

Pisces with Gemini Ascendant

There is great duality inherent in this combination, and sometimes this can cause a few problems. Part of the trouble stems from the fact that you often fail to realise what you want from life, and you could also be accused of failing to take the time out to think things through carefully enough. You are reactive, and although you have every bit of the natural charm that typifies the sign of Gemini, you are more prone to periods of self-doubt and confusion. However, you should not allow these facts to get you down too much, because you are also genuinely loved and have a tremendous capacity to look after others, a factor which is more important to you than any other. It's true that personal relationships can sometimes be a cause of difficulty for you, partly because your constant need to know what makes other people tick could drive them up the wall. Accepting people at face value seems to be the best key to happiness of a personal sort, and there are occasions when your very real and natural intuition has to be put on hold.

It's likely that you are an original, particularly in the way you dress. An early rebellious stage often gives way to a more comfortable form of eccentricity. When you are at your best, just about everyone adores you.

Pisces with Cancer Ascendant

A deep, double Water-sign combination this, and it might serve to make you a very misunderstood, though undoubtedly popular, individual. You are anxious to make a good impression, probably too keen under certain circumstances, and you do everything you can to help others, even if you don't know them very well. It's true that you are deeply sensitive and quite easily brought to tears by the suffering of this most imperfect world that we inhabit. Fatigue can be a problem, though this is somewhat nullified by the fact that you can withdraw completely into the deep recesses of your own mind when it becomes necessary to do so.

You may not be the most gregarious person in the world, simply because it isn't easy for you to put some of your most important considerations into words. This is easier when you are in the company of people you know and trust, though even trust is a commodity that is difficult for you to find, particularly since you may have been hurt by being too willing to share your thoughts early in life. With age comes wisdom and maturity, and the older you are, the better you will learn to handle this potent and demanding combination. You will never go short of either friends or would-be lovers, and may be one of the most magnetic types of both Pisces and Cancer.

Pisces with Leo Ascendant

You are a very sensitive soul, on occasions too much so for your own good. However, there is not a better advocate for the rights of humanity than you represent and you constantly do what you can to support the downtrodden and oppressed. Good causes are your thing and there are likely to be many in your life. You will probably find yourself pushed to the front of almost any enterprise of which you are a part because, despite the deeper qualities of Pisces, you are a natural leader. Even on those occasions when it feels as though you lack confidence, you manage to muddle through somehow and your smile is as broad as the day. Few sign combinations are more loved than this one, mainly because you do not have a malicious bone in your body, and will readily forgive and forget, which the Lion on its own often will not.

Although you are capable of acting on impulse, you do so from a deep sense of moral conviction, so that most of your endeavours are designed to suit other people too. They recognise this fact and will push much support back in your direction. Even when you come across troubles in your life you manage to find ways to sort them out, and will invariably notice something new to smile about on the way. Your sensitivity rating is massive and you can easily be moved to tears.

Pisces with Virgo Ascendant

You might have been accused on occasions of being too sensitive for your own good, a charge that is not entirely without foundation. Certainly you are very understanding of the needs of others, sometimes to the extent that you put everything aside to help them. This would also be true in the case of charities, for you care very much about the world and the people who cling tenaciously to its surface. Your ability to love on a one-to-one basis knows no bounds, though you may not discriminate as much as you could, particularly when young, and might have one or two false starts in the love stakes. You don't always choose to verbalise your thoughts and this can cause problems, because there is always so much going on in your mind and Virgo especially needs good powers of communication. Pisces is quieter and you need to force yourself to say what you think when the explanation is important.

You would never betray a confidence and sometimes take on rather more for the sake of your friends than is strictly good for you. This is not a fault but can cause you problems all the same. Because you are so intuitive there is little that escapes your attention, though you should avoid being pessimistic about your insights. Changes of scenery suit you and travel would bring out the best in what can be a repressed nature.

Pisces with Libra Ascendant

An Air and Water combination, you are not easy to understand and have depths that show at times, surprising those people who thought they already knew what you were. You will always keep people guessing and are just as likely to hitchhike around Europe as you are to hold down a steady job, both of which you would undertake with the same degree of commitment and success. Usually young at heart, but always carrying the potential for an old head on young shoulders, you are something of a paradox and not at all easy for totally 'straight' types to understand. But you always make an impression, and tend to be very attractive to members of the opposite sex.

In matters of health you do have to be a little careful because you dissipate much nervous energy and can sometimes be inclined to push yourself too hard, at least in a mental sense. Frequent periods of rest and meditation will do you the world of good and should improve your level of wisdom, which tends to be fairly high already. Much of your effort in life is expounded on behalf of humanity as a whole, for you care deeply, love totally and always give of your best. Whatever your faults and failings might be, you are one of the most popular people around.

Pisces with Scorpio Ascendant

You stand a chance of disappearing so deep into yourself that other people would need one of those long ladders that cave explorers use to even find you. It isn't really your fault, because both Scorpio and Pisces, as Water signs, are difficult to understand and you have them both. But that doesn't mean that you should be content to remain in the dark, and the warmth of your nature is all you need to shine a light on the wonderful qualities you possess. But the primary word of warning is that you must put yourself on display and allow others to know what you are, before their appreciation of these facts becomes apparent.

As a server of the world you are second to none and it is hard to find a person with this combination who is not, in some way, looking out for the people around them. Immensely attractive to others, you are also one of the most sought-after lovers. Much of this has to do with your deep and abiding charm, but the air of mystery that surrounds you also helps. Some of you will marry too early, and end up regretting the fact, though the majority of people with Scorpio and Pisces will find the love they deserve in the end. You are able, just, firm but fair, though a sucker for a hard luck story and as kind as the day is long. It's hard to imagine how so many good points could be ignored by others.

Pisces with Sagittarius Ascendant

A very attractive combination this, because the more dominant qualities of the Archer are somehow mellowed-out by the caring Water-sign qualities of the Fishes. You can be very outgoing, but there is always a deeper side to your nature that allows others to know that you are thinking about them. Few people could fall out with either your basic nature or your attitude to the world at large, even though there are depths to your nature that may not be easily understood. You are capable, have a good executive ability and can work hard to achieve your objectives, even if you get a little disillusioned on the way. Much of your life is given over to helping those around you and there is a great tendency for you to work for and on behalf of humanity as a whole. A sense of community is brought to most of what you do and you enjoy co-operation. Although you have the natural ability to attract people to you, the Pisces half of your nature makes you just a little more reserved in personal matters than might otherwise be the case. More careful in your choices than either sign taken alone, you still have to make certain that your motivations when commencing a personal relationship are the right ones. You love to be happy, and to offer gifts of happiness to others.

Pisces with Capricorn Ascendant

You are certainly not the easiest person in the world to understand, mainly because your nature is so deep and your personality so complicated, that others are somewhat intimidated at the prospect of staring into this abyss. All the same your friendly nature is attractive, and there will always be people around who are fascinated by the sheer magnetic quality that is intrinsic to this zodiac mix. Sentimental and extremely kind, there is no limit to the extent of your efforts on behalf of a deserving world, though there are some people around who wonder at your commitment and who may ridicule you a little for your staying-power, even in the face of some adversity. At work you are very capable, will work long and hard, and can definitely expect a greater degree of financial and practical success than Pisces when taken alone. Routines don't bother you too much, though you do need regular periods of introspection, which help to recharge low batteries and a battered self-esteem. In affairs of the heart you are given to impulse, which belies the more careful qualities of Capricorn. However, the determination remains intact and you are quite capable of chasing rainbows round and round the same field, never realising that you can't get to the end of them. Generally speaking you are an immensely lovable person and a great favourite to many.

Pisces with Aquarius Ascendant

Here we find the originality of Aquarius balanced by the very sensitive qualities of Pisces, and it makes for a very interesting combination. When it comes to understanding other people you are second to none, but it's certain that you are more instinctive than either Pisces or Aquarius when taken alone. You are better at routines than Aquarius, but also relish a challenge more than the typical Piscean would. Active and enterprising, you tend to know what you want from life, but consideration of others, and the world at large, will always be part of the scenario. People with this combination often work on behalf of humanity and are to be found in social work, the medical profession and religious institutions. As far as beliefs are concerned you don't conform to established patterns, and yet may get closer to the truth of the Creator than many deep theological thinkers have ever been able to do. Acting on impulse as much as you do means that not everyone understands the way your mind works, but your popularity will invariably see you through.

Passionate and deeply sensitive, you are able to negotiate the twists and turns of a romantic life that is hardly likely to be run-of-the-mill. In the end, however, you should certainly be able to find a very deep personal and spiritual happiness.

THE MOON AND THE PART IT PLAYS IN YOUR LIFE

In astrology the Moon is probably the single most important heavenly body after the Sun. Its unique position, as partner to the Earth on its journey around the solar system, means that the Moon appears to pass through the signs of the zodiac extremely quickly. The zodiac position of the Moon at the time of your birth plays a great part in personal character and is especially significant in the build-up of your emotional nature.

Your Own Moon Sign

Discovering the position of the Moon at the time of your birth has always been notoriously difficult because tracking the complex zodiac positions of the Moon is not easy. This process has been reduced to three simple stages with our Lunar Tables. A breakdown of the Moon's zodiac positions can be found from page 35 onwards, so that once you know what your Moon Sign is, you can see what part this plays in the overall build-up of your personal character.

If you follow the instructions on the next page you will soon be able to work out exactly what zodiac sign the Moon occupied on the day that you were born and you can then go on to compare the reading for this position with those of your Sun sign and your Ascendant. It is partly the comparison between these three important positions that goes towards making you the unique individual you are.

How To Discover Your Moon Sign

This is a three-stage process. You may need a pen and a piece of paper but if you follow the instructions below the process should only take a minute or so.

STAGE 1 First of all you need to know the Moon Age at the time of your birth. If you look at Moon Table 1, on page 33, you will find all the years between 1921 and 2019 down the left side. Find the year of your birth and then trace across to the right to the month of your birth. Where the two intersect you will find a number. This is the date of the New Moon in the month that you were born. You now need to count forward the number of days between the New Moon and your own birthday. For example, if the New Moon in the month of your birth was shown as being the 6th and you were born on the 20th, your Moon Age Day would be 14. If the New Moon in the month of your birth came after your birthday, you need to count forward from the New Moon in the previous month. If you were born in a Leap Year, remember to count the 29th February. Whatever the result, jot this number down so that you do not forget it.

STAGE 2 Take a look at Moon Table 2 on page 34. Down the left hand column look for the date of your birth. Now trace across to the month of your birth. Where the two meet you will find a letter. Copy this letter down alongside your Moon Age Day.

STAGE 3 Moon Table 3 on page 34 will supply you with the zodiac sign the Moon occupied on the day of your birth. Look for your Moon Age Day down the left hand column and then for the letter you found in Stage 2. Where the two converge you will find a zodiac sign and this is the sign occupied by the Moon on the day that you were born.

Your Zodiac Moon Sign Explained

You will find a profile of all zodiac Moon Signs on pages 35 to 38, showing in yet another way how astrology helps to make you into the individual that you are. In each daily entry of the Astral Diary you can find the zodiac position of the Moon for every day of the year. This also allows you to discover your lunar birthdays. Since the Moon passes through all the signs of the zodiac in about a month, you can expect something like twelve lunar birthdays each year. At these times you are likely to be emotionally steady and able to make the sort of decisions that have real, lasting value.

MOON TABLE 1

YEAR	JAN	FEB	MAR	YEAR	JAN	FEB	MAR	YEAR	JAN	FEB	MAR
1921	9	8	9	1954	5	3	5	1987	29	28	29
1922	27	26	28	1955	24	22	24	1988	18	17	18
1923	17	15	17	1956	13	11	12	1989	7	6	7
1924	6	5	5	1957	1/30–		1/31	1990	26	25	26
1925	24	23	24	1958	19	18	20	1991	15	14	15
1926	14	12	14	1959	9	7	9	1992	4	3	4
1927	3	2	3	1960	27	26	27	1993	24	22	24
1928	21	19	21	1961	16	15	16	1994	11	10	12
1929	11	9	11	1962	6	5	6	1995	1/31	29	30
1930	29	28	30	1963	25	23	25	1996	19	18	19
1931	18	17	19	1964	14	13	14	1997	9	7	9
1932	7	6	7	1965	3	1	2	1998	27	26	27
1933	25	24	26	1966	21	19	21	1999	16	15	16
1934	15	14	15	1967	10	9	10	2000	6	4	6
1935	5	3	5	1968	29	28	29	2001	24	23	25
1936	24	22	23	1969	19	17	18	2002	13	12	13
1937	12	11	12	1970	7	6	7	2003	3	1	2
1938	1/31–		2/31	1971	26	25	26	2004	21	20	21
1939	20	19	20	1972	15	14	15	2005	10	9	10
1940	9	8	9	1973	5	4	5	2006	29	28	29
1941	27	26	27	1974	24	22	24	2007	18	16	18
1942	16	15	16	1975	12	11	12	2008	8	6	7
1943	6	4	6	1976	1/31	29	30	2009	26	25	26
1944	25	24	24	1977	19	18	19	2010	15	14	15
1945	14	12	14	1978	9	7	9	2011	4	3	5
1946	3	2	3	1979	27	26	27	2012	23	22	22
1947	21	19	21	1980	16	15	16	2013	12	10	12
1948	11	9	11	1981	6	4	6	2014	1/31 –		1
1949	29	27	29	1982	25	23	24	2015	19	20	19
1950	18	16	18	1983	14	13	14	2016	9	8	8
1951	7	6	7	1984	3	1	2	2017	27	25	27
1952	26	25	25	1985	21	19	21	2018	16	15	17
1953	15	14	15	1986	10	9	10	2019	5	4	6

TABLE 2

DAY	FEB	MAR
1	D	F
2	D	G
3	D	G
4	D	G
5	D	G
6	D	G
7	D	G
8	D	G
9	D	G
10	E	G
11	E	G
12	E	H
13	E	H
14	E	H
15	E	H
16	E	H
17	E	H
18	E	H
19	E	H
20	F	H
21	F	H
22	F	I
23	F	I
24	F	I
25	F	I
26	F	I
27	F	I
28	F	I
29	F	I
30	–	I
31	–	I

MOON TABLE 3

M/D	D	E	F	G	H	I	J
0	AQ	PI	PI	PI	AR	AR	AR
1	PI	PI	PI	AR	AR	AR	TA
2	PI	PI	AR	AR	AR	TA	TA
3	PI	AR	AR	AR	TA	TA	TA
4	AR	AR	AR	TA	TA	GE	GE
5	AR	TA	TA	TA	GE	GE	GE
6	TA	TA	TA	GE	GE	GE	CA
7	TA	TA	GE	GE	GE	CA	CA
8	TA	GE	GE	GE	CA	CA	CA
9	GE	GE	CA	CA	CA	CA	LE
10	GE	CA	CA	CA	LE	LE	LE
11	CA	CA	CA	LE	LE	LE	VI
12	CA	CA	LE	LE	LE	VI	VI
13	LE	LE	LE	LE	VI	VI	VI
14	LE	LE	VI	VI	VI	LI	LI
15	LE	VI	VI	VI	LI	LI	LI
16	VI	VI	VI	LI	LI	LI	SC
17	VI	VI	LI	LI	LI	SC	SC
18	VI	LI	LI	LI	SC	SC	SC
19	LI	LI	LI	SC	SC	SC	SA
20	LI	SC	SC	SC	SA	SA	SA
21	SC	SC	SC	SA	SA	SA	CP
22	SC	SC	SA	SA	SA	CP	CP
23	SC	SA	SA	SA	CP	CP	CP
24	SA	SA	SA	CP	CP	CP	AQ
25	SA	CP	CP	CP	AQ	AQ	AQ
26	CP	CP	CP	AQ	AQ	AQ	PI
27	CP	AQ	AQ	AQ	AQ	PI	PI
28	AQ	AQ	AQ	AQ	PI	PI	PI
29	AQ	AQ	AQ	PI	PI	PI	AR

AR = Aries, TA = Taurus, GE = Gemini, CA = Cancer, LE = Leo, VI = Virgo,
LI = Libra, SC = Scorpio, SA = Sagittarius, CP = Capricorn, AQ = Aquarius, PI = Pisces

MOON SIGNS

Moon in Aries

You have a strong imagination, courage, determination and a desire to do things in your own way and forge your own path through life.

Originality is a key attribute; you are seldom stuck for ideas although your mind is changeable and you could take the time to focus on individual tasks. Often quick-tempered, you take orders from few people and live life at a fast pace. Avoid health problems by taking regular time out for rest and relaxation.

Emotionally, it is important that you talk to those you are closest to and work out your true feelings. Once you discover that people are there to help, there is less necessity for you to do everything yourself.

Moon in Taurus

The Moon in Taurus gives you a courteous and friendly manner, which means you are likely to have many friends.

The good things in life mean a lot to you, as Taurus is an Earth sign that delights in experiences which please the senses. Hence you are probably a lover of good food and drink, which may in turn mean you need to keep an eye on the bathroom scales, especially as looking good is also important to you.

Emotionally you are fairly stable and you stick by your own standards. Taureans do not respond well to change. Intuition also plays an important part in your life.

Moon in Gemini

You have a warm-hearted character, sympathetic and eager to help others. At times reserved, you can also be articulate and chatty: this is part of the paradox of Gemini, which always brings duplicity to the nature. You are interested in current affairs, have a good intellect, and are good company and likely to have many friends. Most of your friends have a high opinion of you and would be ready to defend you should the need arise. However, this is usually unnecessary, as you are quite capable of defending yourself in any verbal confrontation.

Travel is important to your inquisitive mind and you find intellectual stimulus in mixing with people from different cultures. You also gain much from reading, writing and the arts but you do need plenty of rest and relaxation in order to avoid fatigue.

Moon in Cancer

The Moon in Cancer at the time of birth is a fortunate position as Cancer is the Moon's natural home. This means that the qualities of compassion and understanding given by the Moon are especially enhanced in your nature, and you are friendly and sociable and cope well with emotional pressures. You cherish home and family life, and happily do the domestic tasks. Your surroundings are important to you and you hate squalor and filth. You are likely to have a love of music and poetry.

Your basic character, although at times changeable like the Moon itself, depends on symmetry. You aim to make your surroundings comfortable and harmonious, for yourself and those close to you.

Moon in Leo

The best qualities of the Moon and Leo come together to make you warm-hearted, fair, ambitious and self-confident. With good organisational abilities, you invariably rise to a position of responsibility in your chosen career. This is fortunate as you don't enjoy being an 'also-ran' and would rather be an important part of a small organisation than a menial in a large one.

You should be lucky in love, and happy, provided you put in the effort to make a comfortable home for yourself and those close to you. It is likely that you will have a love of pleasure, sport, music and literature. Life brings you many rewards, most of them as a direct result of your own efforts, although you may be luckier than average and ready to make the best of any situation.

Moon in Virgo

You are endowed with good mental abilities and a keen receptive memory, but you are never ostentatious or pretentious. Naturally quite reserved, you still have many friends, especially of the opposite sex. Marital relationships must be discussed carefully and worked at so that they remain harmonious, as personal attachments can be a problem if you do not give them your full attention.

Talented and persevering, you possess artistic qualities and are a good homemaker. Earning your honours through genuine merit, you work long and hard towards your objectives but show little pride in your achievements. Many short journeys will be undertaken in your life.

Moon in Libra

With the Moon in Libra you are naturally popular and make friends easily. People like you, probably more than you realise, you bring fun to a party and are a natural diplomat. For all its good points, Libra is not the most stable of astrological signs and, as a result, your emotions can be a little unstable too. Therefore, although the Moon in Libra is said to be good for love and marriage, your Sun sign and Rising sign will have an important effect on your emotional and loving qualities.

You must remember to relate to others in your decision-making. Co-operation is crucial because Libra represents the 'balance' of life that can only be achieved through harmonious relationships. Conformity is not easy for you because Libra, an Air sign, likes its independence.

Moon in Scorpio

Some people might call you pushy. In fact, all you really want to do is to live life to the full and protect yourself and your family from the pressures of life. Take care to avoid giving the impression of being sarcastic or impulsive and use your energies wisely and constructively.

You have great courage and you invariably achieve your goals by force of personality and sheer effort. You are fond of mystery and are good at predicting the outcome of situations and events. Travel experiences can be beneficial to you.

You may experience problems if you do not take time to examine your motives in a relationship, and also if you allow jealousy, always a feature of Scorpio, to cloud your judgement.

Moon in Sagittarius

The Moon in Sagittarius helps to make you a generous individual with humanitarian qualities and a kind heart. Restlessness may be intrinsic as your mind is seldom still. Perhaps because of this, you have a need for change that could lead you to several major moves during your adult life. You are not afraid to stand your ground when you know your judgement is right, you speak directly and have good intuition.

At work you are quick, efficient and versatile and so you make an ideal employee. You need work to be intellectually demanding and do not enjoy tedious routines.

In relationships, you anger quickly if faced with stupidity or deception, though you are just as quick to forgive and forget. Emotionally, there are times when your heart rules your head.

Moon in Capricorn

The Moon in Capricorn makes you popular and likely to come into the public eye in some way. The watery Moon is not entirely comfortable in the Earth sign of Capricorn and this may lead to some difficulties in the early years of life. An initial lack of creative ability and indecision must be overcome before the true qualities of patience and perseverance inherent in Capricorn can show through.

You have good administrative ability and are a capable worker, and if you are careful you can accumulate wealth. But you must be cautious and take professional advice in partnerships, as you are open to deception. You may be interested in social or welfare work, which suit your organisational skills and sympathy for others.

Moon in Aquarius

The Moon in Aquarius makes you an active and agreeable person with a friendly, easy-going nature. Sympathetic to the needs of others, you flourish in a laid-back atmosphere. You are broad-minded, fair and open to suggestion, although sometimes you have an unconventional quality which others can find hard to understand.

You are interested in the strange and curious, and in old articles and places. You enjoy trips to these places and gain much from them. Political, scientific and educational work interests you and you might choose a career in science or technology.

Money-wise, you make gains through innovation and concentration and Lunar Aquarians often tackle more than one job at a time. In love you are kind and honest.

Moon in Pisces

You have a kind, sympathetic nature, somewhat retiring at times, but you always take account of others' feelings and help when you can.

Personal relationships may be problematic, but as life goes on you can learn from your experiences and develop a better understanding of yourself and the world around you.

You have a fondness for travel, appreciate beauty and harmony and hate disorder and strife. You may be fond of literature and would make a good writer or speaker yourself. You have a creative imagination and may come across as an incurable romantic. You have strong intuition, maybe bordering on a mediumistic quality, which sets you apart from the mass. You may not be rich in cash terms, but your personal gifts are worth more than gold.

PISCES IN LOVE

Discover how compatible in love you are with people from the same and other signs of the zodiac. Five stars equals a match made in heaven!

Pisces meets Pisces

Pisceans are easy-going and get on well with most people, so when two Pisceans get together, harmony is invariably the result. While this isn't the most dynamic relationship, there is mutual understanding, and a desire to please on both sides. Neither partner is likely to be overbearing or selfish. Family responsibilities should be happily shared and home surroundings will be comfortable, but never pretentious. One of the better pairings for the sign of the Fishes. Star rating: *****

Pisces meets Aries

Still waters run deep, and they don't come much deeper than Pisces. Although these signs share the same quadrant of the zodiac, they have little in common. Pisces is a dreamer, a romantic idealist with steady and spiritual goals. Aries needs to be on the move, and has very different ideals. It's hard to see how a relationship could develop but, with patience, there is a chance that things might work out. Pisces needs incentive, and Aries may be the sign to offer it. Star rating: **

Pisces meets Taurus

No problem here, unless both parties come from the quieter side of their respective signs. Most of the time Taurus and Pisces would live comfortably together, offering mutual support and deep regard. Taurus can offer the personal qualities that Pisces craves, whilst Pisces understands and copes with the Bull's slightly stubborn qualities. Taurus is likely to travel in Piscean company, so there is a potential for wide-ranging experiences and variety which is essential. There will be some misunderstandings, mainly because Pisces is so deep, but that won't prevent their enduring happiness. Star rating: ***

Pisces meets Gemini

Gemini likes to think of itself as intuitive and intellectual, but it will never understand Pisces' dark depths. Another stumbling block is that both Gemini and Pisces are 'split' signs – the Twins and the two Fishes – which means that both are capable of dual personalities. There won't be any shortage of affection, but the real question has to be how much these people feel they have in common. Pisces is extremely kind, and so is Gemini most of the time. But Pisces does too much soul-searching for Gemini, who might eventually become bored. Star rating: ***

Pisces meets Cancer

This is likely to be a very successful match. Cancer and Pisces are both Water signs, both deep, sensitive and very caring. Pisces loves deeply, and Cancer wants to be loved. There will be few fireworks here, and a very quiet house. But that doesn't mean that either love or action is lacking – the latter of which is just behind closed doors. Family and children are important to both signs and both are prepared to work hard, but Pisces is the more restless of the two and needs the support and security that Cancer offers. Star rating: *****

Pisces meets Leo

Pisces always needs to understand others, which makes Leo feel warm and loved, while Leo sees, to its delight, that Pisces needs to be protected and taken care of. Pisceans are often lacking in self-confidence which is something Leo has to spare, and happily it is often infectious. Pisces' inevitable cares are swept away on a tide of Leonine cheerfulness. This couple's home would be cheerful and full of love, which is beneficial to all family members. This is not a meeting of minds, but rather an understanding and appreciation of differences. Star rating: ****

Pisces meets Virgo

This looks an unpromising match from beginning to end. There are exceptions to every rule, particularly where Pisces is concerned, but these two signs are both so deep it's hard to imagine that they could ever find what makes the other tick. The depth is different in each case: Virgo's ruminations are extremely materialistic, while Pisces exists in a world of deep-felt, poorly expressed emotion. Pisces and Virgo might find they don't talk much, so only in a contemplative, almost monastic, match would they ever get on. Still, in a vast zodiac, anything is possible. Star rating: **

Pisces meets Libra

Libra and Pisces can be extremely fond of each other, even deeply in love, but this alone isn't a stable foundation for long-term success. Pisces is extremely deep and doesn't even know itself very well. Libra may initially find this intriguing but will eventually feel frustrated at being unable to understand the Piscean's emotional and personal feelings. Pisces can be jealous and may find Libra's flightiness difficult, which Libra can't stand. They are great friends and they may make it to the romantic stakes, but when they get there a great deal of effort will be necessary. Star rating: ***

Pisces meets Scorpio

If ever there were two zodiac signs that have a total rapport, it has to be Scorpio and Pisces. They share very similar needs: they are not gregarious and are happy with a little silence, good music and time to contemplate the finer things in life, and both are attracted to family life. Apart, they can have a tendency to wander in a romantic sense, but this is reduced when they come together. They are deep, firm friends who enjoy each other's company and this must lead to an excellent chance of success. These people are surely made for each other! Star rating: *****

Pisces meets Sagittarius

Probably the least likely success story for either sign, which is why it scores so low on the star rating. The basic problem is an almost total lack of understanding. A successful relationship needs empathy and progress towards a shared goal but, although both are eager to please, Pisces is too deep and Sagittarius too flighty – they just don't belong on the same planet! As pals, they have more in common and so a friendship is the best hope of success and happiness. Star rating: *

Pisces meets Capricorn

There is some chance of a happy relationship here, but it will need work on both sides. Capricorn is a go-getter, but likes to plan long term. Pisces is naturally more immediate, but has enough intuition to understand the Goat's thinking. Both have patience, but it will usually be Pisces who chooses to play second fiddle. The quiet nature of both signs might be a problem, as someone will have to take the lead, especially in social situations. Both signs should recognise this fact and accommodate it. Star rating: ***

Pisces meets Aquarius

Zodiac signs that follow each other often have something in common, but this is often not the case with Aquarius and Pisces. Both signs are deeply caring, but in different ways. Pisces is one of the deepest zodiac signs, and Aquarius simply isn't prepared to embark on the journey. Pisceans, meanwhile, would probably find Aquarians superficial and even flippant. On the positive side, there is potential for a well-balanced relationship, but unless one party is untypical of their zodiac sign, it often doesn't get started. Star rating: **

VENUS:
THE PLANET OF LOVE

If you look up at the sky around sunset or sunrise you will often see Venus in close attendance to the Sun. It is arguably one of the most beautiful sights of all and there is little wonder that historically it became associated with the goddess of love. But although Venus does play an important part in the way you view love and in the way others see you romantically, this is only one of the spheres of influence that it enjoys in your overall character.

Venus has a part to play in the more cultured side of your life and has much to do with your appreciation of art, literature, music and general creativity. Even the way you look is responsive to the part of the zodiac that Venus occupied at the start of your life, though this fact is also down to your Sun sign and Ascending sign. If, at the time you were born, Venus occupied one of the more gregarious zodiac signs, you will be more likely to wear your heart on your sleeve, as well as to be more attracted to entertainment, social gatherings and good company. If on the other hand Venus occupied a quiet zodiac sign at the time of your birth, you would tend to be more retiring and less willing to shine in public situations.

It's good to know what part the planet Venus plays in your life for it can have a great bearing on the way you appear to the rest of the world and since we all have to mix with others, you can learn to make the very best of what Venus has to offer you.

One of the great complications in the past has always been trying to establish exactly what zodiac position Venus enjoyed when you were born because the planet is notoriously difficult to track. However, we have solved that problem by creating a table that is exclusive to your Sun sign, which you will find on the following page.

Establishing your Venus sign could not be easier. Just look up the year of your birth on the following page and you will see a sign of the zodiac. This was the sign that Venus occupied in the period covered by your sign in that year. If Venus occupied more than one sign during the period, this is indicated by the date on which the sign changed, and the name of the new sign. For instance, if you were born in 1940, Venus was in Aries until the 9th March, after which time it was in Taurus. If you were born before 9th March your Venus sign is Aries, if you were born on or after 9th March, your Venus sign is Taurus. Once you have established the position of Venus at the time of your birth, you can then look in the pages which follow to see how this has a bearing on your life as a whole.

1921 ARIES / 8.3 TAURUS
1922 PISCES / 14.3 ARIES
1923 CAPRICORN
1924 ARIES / 10.3 TAURUS
1925 AQUARIUS / 4.3 PISCES
1926 AQUARIUS
1927 PISCES / 26.2 ARIES
1928 CAPRICORN / 23.2 AQUARIUS /
    18.3 PISCES
1929 ARIES / 9.3 TAURUS
1930 PISCES / 13.3 ARIES
1931 CAPRICORN
1932 ARIES / 9.3 TAURUS
1933 AQUARIUS / 4.3 PISCES
1934 AQUARIUS
1935 PISCES / 25.2 ARIES
1936 CAPRICORN / 23.2 AQUARIUS /
    18.3 PISCES
1937 ARIES / 10.3 TAURUS
1938 PISCES / 12.3 ARIES
1939 CAPRICORN
1940 ARIES / 9.3 TAURUS
1941 AQUARIUS / 3.3 PISCES
1942 AQUARIUS
1943 PISCES / 25.2 ARIES
1944 CAPRICORN / 22.2 AQUARIUS /
    18.3 PISCES
1945 ARIES / 11.3 TAURUS
1946 PISCES / 11.3 ARIES
1947 CAPRICORN
1948 ARIES / 8.3 TAURUS
1949 AQUARIUS / 3.3 PISCES
1950 AQUARIUS
1951 PISCES / 24.2 ARIES
1952 CAPRICORN / 22.2 AQUARIUS /
    17.3 PISCES
1953 ARIES
1954 PISCES / 11.3 ARIES
1955 CAPRICORN
1956 ARIES / 8.3 TAURUS
1957 AQUARIUS / 2.3 PISCES
1958 CAPRICORN / 25.2 AQUARIUS
1959 PISCES / 24.2 ARIES
1960 CAPRICORN / 21.2 AQUARIUS /
    17.3 PISCES
1961 ARIES
1962 PISCES / 10.3 ARIES
1963 CAPRICORN
1964 ARIES / 8.3 TAURUS
1965 AQUARIUS / 1.3 PISCES
1966 AQUARIUS
1967 PISCES / 23.2 ARIES
1968 SAGITTARIUS / 26.1 CAPRICORN
1969 ARIES

1970 PISCES / 10.3 ARIES
1971 CAPRICORN
1972 ARIES / 7.3 TAURUS
1973 AQUARIUS / 1.3 PISCES
1974 CAPRICORN / 2.3 AQUARIUS
1975 PISCES / 23.2 ARIES
1976 SAGITTARIUS / 26.1 CAPRICORN
1977 ARIES
1978 PISCES / 9.3 ARIES
1979 CAPRICORN
1980 ARIES / 7.3 TAURUS
1981 AQUARIUS / 28.2 PISCES
1982 CAPRICORN / 4.3 AQUARIUS
1983 PISCES / 23.2 ARIES
1984 SAGITTARIUS / 25.1 CAPRICORN
1985 ARIES
1986 PISCES / 9.3 ARIES
1987 CAPRICORN
1988 ARIES / 7.3 TAURUS
1989 AQUARIUS / 28.2 PISCES
1990 CAPRICORN / 5.3 AQUARIUS
1991 PISCES / 22.2 ARIES /
    20.3 TAURUS
1992 SAGITTARIUS / 25.1 CAPRICORN
1993 ARIES
1994 PISCES / 9.3 ARIES
1995 CAPRICORN
1996 ARIES / 7.3 TAURUS
1997 AQUARIUS / 27.2 PISCES
1998 CAPRICORN / 5.3 AQUARIUS
1999 PISCES / 22.2 ARIES /
    19.3 TAURUS
2000 SAGITTARIUS / 25.1 CAPRICORN
2001 ARIES
2002 PISCES / 9.3 ARIES
2003 CAPRICORN
2004 ARIES / 7.3 TAURUS
2005 AQUARIUS / 27.2 PISCES
2006 CAPRICORN / 5.3 AQUARIUS
2007 PISCES / 22.2 ARIES
2008 SAGITTARIUS / 25.1 CAPRICORN
2009 ARIES
2010 PISCES / 9.3 ARIES
2011 CAPRICORN
2012 ARIES / 7.3 TAURUS
2013 AQUARIUS / 27.2 PISCES
2014 AQUARIUS / 27.2 PISCES
2015 PISCES / 22.2 ARIES
2016 AQUARIUS / 6.2 PISCES
2017 ARIES
2018 PISCES / 9.3 ARIES
2019 CAPRICORN

VENUS THROUGH THE ZODIAC SIGNS

Venus in Aries

Amongst other things, the position of Venus in Aries indicates a fondness for travel, music and all creative pursuits. Your nature tends to be affectionate and you would try not to create confusion or difficulty for others if it could be avoided. Many people with this planetary position have a great love of the theatre, and mental stimulation is of the greatest importance. Early romantic attachments are common with Venus in Aries, so it is very important to establish a genuine sense of romantic continuity. Early marriage is not recommended, especially if it is based on sympathy. You may give your heart a little too readily on occasions.

Venus in Taurus

You are capable of very deep feelings and your emotions tend to last for a very long time. This makes you a trusting partner and lover, whose constancy is second to none. In life you are precise and careful and always try to do things the right way. Although this means an ordered life, which you are comfortable with, it can also lead you to be rather too fussy for your own good. Despite your pleasant nature, you are very fixed in your opinions and quite able to speak your mind. Others are attracted to you and historical astrologers always quoted this position of Venus as being very fortunate in terms of marriage. However, if you find yourself involved in a failed relationship, it could take you a long time to trust again.

Venus in Gemini

As with all associations related to Gemini, you tend to be quite versatile, anxious for change and intelligent in your dealings with the world at large. You may gain money from more than one source but you are equally good at spending it. There is an inference here that you are a good communicator, via either the written or the spoken word, and you love to be in the company of interesting people. Always on the look-out for culture, you may also be very fond of music, and love to indulge the curious and cultured side of your nature. In romance you tend to have more than one relationship and could find yourself associated with someone who has previously been a friend or even a distant relative.

Venus in Cancer

You often stay close to home because you are very fond of family and enjoy many of your most treasured moments when you are with those you love. Being naturally sympathetic, you will always do anything you can to support those around you, even people you hardly know at all. This charitable side of your nature is your most noticeable trait and is one of the reasons why others are naturally so fond of you. Being receptive and in some cases even psychic, you can see through to the soul of most of those with whom you come into contact. You may not commence too many romantic attachments but when you do give your heart, it tends to be unconditionally.

Venus in Leo

It must become quickly obvious to almost anyone you meet that you are kind, sympathetic and yet determined enough to stand up for anyone or anything that is truly important to you. Bright and sunny, you warm the world with your natural enthusiasm and would rarely do anything to hurt those around you, or at least not intentionally. In romance you are ardent and sincere, though some may find your style just a little overpowering. Gains come through your contacts with other people and this could be especially true with regard to romance, for love and money often come hand in hand for those who were born with Venus in Leo. People claim to understand you, though you are more complex than you seem.

Venus in Virgo

Your nature could well be fairly quiet no matter what your Sun sign might be, though this fact often manifests itself as an inner peace and would not prevent you from being basically sociable. Some delays and even the odd disappointment in love cannot be ruled out with this planetary position, though it's a fact that you will usually find the happiness you look for in the end. Catapulting yourself into romantic entanglements that you know to be rather ill-advised is not sensible, and it would be better to wait before you committed yourself exclusively to any one person. It is the essence of your nature to serve the world at large and through doing so it is possible that you will attract money at some stage in your life.

Venus in Libra

Venus is very comfortable in Libra and bestows upon those people who have this planetary position a particular sort of kindness that is easy to recognise. This is a very good position for all sorts of friendships and also for romantic attachments that usually bring much joy into your life. Few individuals with Venus in Libra would avoid marriage and since you are capable of great depths of love, it is likely that you will find a contented personal life. You like to mix with people of integrity and intelligence but don't take kindly to scruffy surroundings or work that means getting your hands too dirty. Careful speculation, good business dealings and money through marriage all seem fairly likely.

Venus in Scorpio

You are quite open and tend to spend money quite freely, even on those occasions when you don't have very much. Although your intentions are always good, there are times when you get yourself in to the odd scrape and this can be particularly true when it comes to romance, which you may come to late or from a rather unexpected direction. Certainly you have the power to be happy and to make others contented on the way, but you find the odd stumbling block on your journey through life and it could seem that you have to work harder than those around you. As a result of this, you gain a much deeper understanding of the true value of personal happiness than many people ever do, and are likely to achieve true contentment in the end.

Venus in Sagittarius

You are lighthearted, cheerful and always able to see the funny side of any situation. These facts enhance your popularity, which is especially high with members of the opposite sex. You should never have to look too far to find romantic interest in your life, though it is just possible that you might be too willing to commit yourself before you are certain that the person in question is right for you. Part of the problem here extends to other areas of life too. The fact is that you like variety in everything and so can tire of situations that fail to offer it. All the same, if you choose wisely and learn to understand your restless side, then great happiness can be yours.

Venus in Capricorn

The most notable trait that comes from Venus in this position is that it makes you trustworthy and able to take on all sorts of responsibilities in life. People are instinctively fond of you and love you all the more because you are always ready to help those who are in any form of need. Social and business popularity can be yours and there is a magnetic quality to your nature that is particularly attractive in a romantic sense. Anyone who wants a partner for a lover, a spouse and a good friend too would almost certainly look in your direction. Constancy is the hallmark of your nature and unfaithfulness would go right against the grain. You might sometimes be a little too trusting.

Venus in Aquarius

This location of Venus offers a fondness for travel and a desire to try out something new at every possible opportunity. You are extremely easy to get along with and tend to have many friends from varied backgrounds, classes and inclinations. You like to live a distinct sort of life and gain a great deal from moving about, both in a career sense and with regard to your home. It is not out of the question that you could form a romantic attachment to someone who comes from far away or be attracted to a person of a distinctly artistic and original nature. What you cannot stand is jealousy, for you have friends of both sexes and would want to keep things that way.

Venus in Pisces

The first thing people tend to notice about you is your wonderful, warm smile. Being very charitable by nature you will do anything to help others, even if you don't know them well. Much of your life may be spent sorting out situations for other people, but it is very important to feel that you are living for yourself too. In the main, you remain cheerful, and tend to be quite attractive to members of the opposite sex. Where romantic attachments are concerned, you could be drawn to people who are significantly older or younger than yourself or to someone with a unique career or point of view. It might be best for you to avoid marrying whilst you are still very young.

PISCES:
2018 DIARY PAGES

October

2018

1 MONDAY

Moon Age Day 22   Moon Sign Gemini

You are entering a pretty dynamic and competitive phase at work and Pisceans who are not in work at present should definitely be keeping their eyes open now. It isn't out of the question that some Pisceans will be taking a holiday around this time. If so, you have chosen wisely and should have an excellent break.

2 TUESDAY

Moon Age Day 23   Moon Sign Cancer

A personal matter is likely to put you on the defensive today but do make sure you are not defending yourself before you have even been attacked. The people who matter the most will be on your side at the moment and are unlikely to let you down, even if the going gets a little difficult.

3 WEDNESDAY

Moon Age Day 24   Moon Sign Cancer

This should be a potentially wonderful time in terms of personal relationships. There are quite a few planetary aspects and positions now working in your favour and very little to get in the way of romantic bliss. If you are not involved in a personal attachment right now, perhaps you should be keeping your eyes open.

4 THURSDAY

Moon Age Day 25   Moon Sign Leo

If you have to rethink a particular plan of action, don't see this as being necessarily bad. On the contrary, the more you rush into things right now, the greater is the likelihood of making a mistake, so take plenty of time to organise things methodically. People you haven't seen for quite some time could be making a renewed appearance in your life today.

5 FRIDAY
Moon Age Day 26   Moon Sign Leo

This may be the best time of this month to have a clear out in your life. It could be that there are certain business or social relationships that have been holding you back or people who simply don't seem to have your best interests at heart. You are far from being hard-hearted but may be forced by circumstances to look again at situations.

6 SATURDAY
Moon Age Day 27   Moon Sign Virgo

This certainly isn't the most progressive day of the month. The lunar low can make you feel sluggish and could see you putting off something you have been planning for a while. Make the day your own by doing exactly what takes your fancy. If that means curling up with a book, then so be it.

7 SUNDAY
Moon Age Day 28   Moon Sign Virgo

Major decisions are left until later. You are not really in a position to take chances at the moment and might regret it if you do. For the moment, simply coast along and watch others setting the pace. You should be able to get a good deal from friendships and pastimes that you always enjoy so focus on these for now.

8 MONDAY
Moon Age Day 29   Moon Sign Virgo

Any outdoor pursuits you may follow are especially well highlighted now, as the more sporting and competitive side of your nature also beings to show itself. Because you are feeling brave at present, you may choose to tackle an issue that has had you quaking in your boots at some stage in the past.

9 TUESDAY
Moon Age Day 0   Moon Sign Libra

This may be the time to bring something to a successful conclusion – this inclination has been around in your chart for the last few days but it looks even more pertinent now. Be on the lookout for ways to improve your life and also your finances. A change of scene would probably be welcome.

10 WEDNESDAY
Moon Age Day 1   Moon Sign Libra

It can benefit you greatly to keep in touch with people who are in the know. Because of your generally affable ways, people like you a great deal. Turn this fact to your advantage for once and call in some assistance. Moving towards the culmination of plans you hatched some time ago, you make material progress.

11 THURSDAY
Moon Age Day 2   Moon Sign Scorpio

With a greater sense of freedom and adventure than you have experienced for some weeks, it looks as though this part of October is turning very much to your advantage. What you find within yourself right now is greater confidence and a desire to get on well, both practically and socially.

12 FRIDAY
Moon Age Day 3   Moon Sign Scorpio

Your potential for personal freedom is very strong. This can make you something of a loose cannon on occasions because people who think they know you well are likely to be constantly surprised by your actions and reactions. It doesn't do any harm at all to keep the world guessing once in a while.

13 SATURDAY
Moon Age Day 4   Moon Sign Sagittarius

Some emotional issues can seem to be more trouble than they are worth but it may be that a crucial issue between yourself and someone you love simply has to receive an airing at this time. Of course, you will be as tactful as always but you simply cannot leave things alone to possibly deteriorate further.

14 SUNDAY
Moon Age Day 5   Moon Sign Sagittarius

This is a marvellous period to get out into the world of social interaction and to make certain that your voice is heard. You will be making some new contacts this Sunday, most likely people who will become firm friends and who are in a good position to offer you some timely support.

15 MONDAY   *Moon Age Day 6   Moon Sign Capricorn*

Close, emotional involvement should now prove more satisfying than ever. This is not likely to be a quiet Monday but it does offer you the chance to show loved ones how important they are to you. Your sense of balance is good and you will instinctively know how and when to offer the best advice.

16 TUESDAY   *Moon Age Day 7   Moon Sign Capricorn*

You now decide to get down to the real nitty-gritty of life and you won't have any trouble at all convincing your family and friends that the decisions you make are the best ones in an all-round sense. Love is high on your agenda and you manage to find exactly the right words to please your partner now.

17 WEDNESDAY   *Moon Age Day 8   Moon Sign Capricorn*

Weigh up specific options carefully because it is entirely possible to make significant mistakes today if you rush into anything. Getting on side with someone who has proved to be difficult in the past should now be easier, mainly because your own frame of mind is very adaptable at present.

18 THURSDAY   *Moon Age Day 9   Moon Sign Aquarius*

Professionally speaking, you may decide that you cannot afford to miss out on anything today. Throw your efforts into opportunities at work, but not to the exclusion of all else. You should also be able to find plenty of diversion coming from the direction of friends, many of whom definitely have your best interests at heart.

19 FRIDAY   *Moon Age Day 10   Moon Sign Aquarius*

This would be a good time to join forces with friends or maybe neighbours in order to sort out something you are definitely not happy about. Pisces is a natural crusader, especially against unfairness of any sort. Outside of work you may find that you have far less time for personal enjoyment today than you might have wished.

20 SATURDAY   *Moon Age Day 11   Moon Sign Pisces*

This is a day of high energy and maximum achievement. Catapulted out of any twelfth house moon lethargy, you now surge forward positively, making for a potentially interesting and eventful weekend. Confusion of any sort is blown away by a necessary and welcome wind of change.

21 SUNDAY   *Moon Age Day 12   Moon Sign Pisces*

Getting your own way with others ought to be a piece of cake at the moment. With a natural sense of good luck, together with poise, balance and a determination to get on well, very little should be denied you this Sunday. The thing to avoid is staying around at home with nothing particular to do.

22 MONDAY   *Moon Age Day 13   Moon Sign Pisces*

Making any sort of important change is likely to be quite easy today, though you may have to deal with the slightly odd behaviour of a few of the people you are relying on at this time. Controversy is likely at some stage during the day, even if you are not the one who is inspiring it.

23 TUESDAY   *Moon Age Day 14   Moon Sign Aries*

You can get a great deal out of journeys of any sort and although the summer is now over, you might decide that the time is right to take a holiday. Travel that is organised at very short notice could be the most enjoyable of all and you can also gain from mixing with people who come from far away.

24 WEDNESDAY   *Moon Age Day 15   Moon Sign Aries*

Success right now has a great deal to do with the influence you have over others. You may have to change your mind about something you thought you understood well but you won't lose credibility if you are able to explain yourself. Controversy can still dog your footsteps, this time maybe in terms of your personal life.

25 THURSDAY   *Moon Age Day 16   Moon Sign Taurus*

Contact with a variety of different sorts of people really makes life go with a swing and you cannot afford to hide either your nature or your talents at present. If you are good at something, now is the time to show the fact to the world at large. Romance could be on the cards for both young and young-at-heart Pisceans.

26 FRIDAY   *Moon Age Day 17   Moon Sign Taurus*

A personal plan or a specific intention on your part may now have to be scrapped, probably through no fault of your own. If this leads to some disappointment, the best way forward is to forget about a situation that is in the past and to pull even harder for the winning post in other ways. People make a fuss of you later today.

27 SATURDAY   *Moon Age Day 18   Moon Sign Gemini*

You should let your personality shine out this weekend because there are plenty of people watching you, some of whom are deeply attracted to that Piscean nature of yours. Don't be too modest and when you are asked for your opinion, do your best to act as though you have the right to offer it.

28 SUNDAY   *Moon Age Day 19   Moon Sign Gemini*

Ideas could fail to turn out quite as you had expected and that could mean having to alter your strategy at a moment's notice. This shouldn't present you with too many problems, since your mind is working quickly and you don't have too much trouble thinking on your feet under present astrological trends.

29 MONDAY   *Moon Age Day 20   Moon Sign Cancer*

There are planets around now that emphasise your obligations to others, which might be something of a drag during one of those few occasions for Pisces that you are thinking about yourself. It won't be long before a particularly tedious job is out of the way, which should leave you with more time to do what you want.

30 TUESDAY *Moon Age Day 21   Moon Sign Cancer*

Seek change and variety for its own sake today and don't allow yourself to be held to one spot or a particular way of thinking. There are some gains to be made, not least of all in terms of the way you are looking at romantic matters. However, don't get sucked into the crazy schemes of someone you already fear could be a control-freak.

31 WEDNESDAY *Moon Age Day 22   Moon Sign Cancer*

Socially speaking, this should be a very beneficial period. Present influences can bring you into contact with people from many different walks of life. Your horizons will be broadened immensely and it looks as though you have extra energy when you need it the most. Best of all, romance shines brightly in your life.

November
2018

1 THURSDAY
Moon Age Day 23   Moon Sign Leo

The first day of November could represent a good time for some sort of professional accomplishment. Certain matters that have been on hold for a while could come to fruition now and the chance of making money is quite good. Friends may have special needs of you around this time.

2 FRIDAY
Moon Age Day 24   Moon Sign Leo

Social highlights are present in your chart, making this a very good time for having fun and for making new friends. There are a number of confidences coming your way right now and it is very important that you guard these carefully since your reputation with some might rest on your discretion.

3 SATURDAY
Moon Age Day 25   Moon Sign Virgo

You have really been pushing hard this week and such is your momentum that it will carry you well into the lunar low before you even recognise its presence. All the same, it might be advisable to ease off somewhat, particularly when it comes to taking unnecessary and perhaps slightly foolish chances.

4 SUNDAY
Moon Age Day 26   Moon Sign Virgo

If there is a problem around today, it could well be your over-emotional tendencies. You would be well advised to use practical common sense, rather than to allow your naturally kind ways to influence your judgement. Someone could be out to take you for a ride, but not if you pay attention to what they are doing.

5 MONDAY
Moon Age Day 27   Moon Sign Libra

This is a period during which you should be getting as much rest as possible. It isn't that any trends are working against your best interests but simply that you have reached the end of a particular phase and need to take a break before starting on something else. From a personal viewpoint, today should find you very content.

6 TUESDAY
Moon Age Day 28   Moon Sign Libra

There are some new and interesting people around at the moment. If you haven't already taken this fact into account, maybe you should do so today. Whether you meet these people at work, or within your home-life, you can get a great deal out of new encounters. These should furnish you with schemes and plans for next year.

7 WEDNESDAY
Moon Age Day 0   Moon Sign Scorpio

You can make today very interesting for yourself but there are a few small setbacks to take into account. It is possible that in the middle of enjoying yourself, there will be a number of people around who have it in mind that you should be working. If you become aware of this you are likely to feel it is an injustice – and even Pisces fights back sometimes.

8 THURSDAY
Moon Age Day 1   Moon Sign Scorpio

You are out there in the social mainstream today, even if that is not exactly where you planned on being. On every level, work takes something of a back seat in favour of having fun for a little while. Your confidence is far from lacking, especially when you are in the company of people who naturally make you feel good.

9 FRIDAY
Moon Age Day 2   Moon Sign Sagittarius

You are still in a go-ahead frame of mind but you manifest this slightly differently now. If someone is needed to cheer up a really sad individual, then that person is definitely you. Your sense of humour is especially infectious and you have a natural wisdom that hardly anyone could fail to recognise.

10 SATURDAY   *Moon Age Day 3   Moon Sign Sagittarius*

You feel the need to broaden your horizons as much as possible today, so avoid being in any way restricted in your thinking. Pisces is full of very creative ideas around now, a factor that can stand you in good stead, both at home and work. Keep abreast of current affairs to broaden your mind, too.

11 SUNDAY   *Moon Age Day 4   Moon Sign Sagittarius*

The opportunities for overall gain are good today, though you could find yourself so keen on breaking down barriers and achieving more personal freedom that you don't address the financial aspect of life at all. Avoid listening to either rumours or gossip, both of which are likely to give you false information.

12 MONDAY   *Moon Age Day 5   Moon Sign Capricorn*

This is a good day from a professional point of view and it is easy to make allies at every stage. A continued reliance on a certain individual could lead to one or two problems, especially if the person concerned fails to live up to your expectations. Embark on new projects with as much confidence as you can muster.

13 TUESDAY   *Moon Age Day 6   Moon Sign Capricorn*

Contacts with superiors at work might lead to a better understanding and could even prove advantageous to you personally in the fullness of time. A task to which there seems to have been no end should be drawing to a close before very long, leaving you with more time to do other things.

14 WEDNESDAY   *Moon Age Day 7   Moon Sign Aquarius*

Don't expect life to organise itself, particularly at work. You may have to pitch in early in the day, possibly to sort out a mess made by someone else. With good humour and the understanding that is born into Pisces people, you attend to things today and maintain a happy frame of mind.

15 THURSDAY   *Moon Age Day 8   Moon Sign Aquarius*

It is easier to address the needs and wants of loved ones today, rather than spending too much time thinking about what you want for yourself. This is the truly unselfish quality of Pisces, which is never really very far from the surface. Your intuition works well when you are dealing with strangers.

16 FRIDAY   *Moon Age Day 9   Moon Sign Aquarius*

Current trends leave you with some new directions to travel, either in a real or a figurative sense. You might not be feeling particularly brave at present but this doesn't show and just about everyone you meet is impressed with you. Don't be too quick to step aside in favour of someone else if there is something you really want.

17 SATURDAY   ☿   *Moon Age Day 10   Moon Sign Pisces*

The Moon returns to your sign and brings with it what is potentially the most outgoing and fun-loving period of the month. You articulate your needs and wants particularly well and know how to make it possible for those around you to have an especially good and enjoyable time. Enjoy the buzz.

18 SUNDAY   ☿   *Moon Age Day 11   Moon Sign Pisces*

This is the high point in maintaining the sort of progress more normally associated with the Fire-signs in the zodiac, such as Aries. Although you fortunately fail to manifest the more selfish aspects of some of your more gregarious zodiac cousins, you certainly know how to paint the town red at the moment.

19 MONDAY   ☿   *Moon Age Day 12   Moon Sign Aries*

You should prepare yourself for some heart-warming surprises and for a few gains that you didn't expect. Everyday matters bring the results you have been expecting and probably more besides. With a positive and useful week ahead, you may decide to start enjoying yourself long before today is over.

20 TUESDAY ☿ *Moon Age Day 13* *Moon Sign Aries*

You will be attending to a number of different jobs today but like the juggler you are it is possible to keep all the balls in the air at the same time. Not everyone believes in you right now but the people who matter the most will and that fact is enough to see you through one or two potentially sticky moments.

21 WEDNESDAY ☿ *Moon Age Day 14* *Moon Sign Taurus*

You should find yourself on the right side of some interesting situations today, even if you have to dream them up for yourself. Not everyone displays the same sort of sense of humour that you do right now but that doesn't matter because you will make them laugh in one way or another. Look after cash in the afternoon and evening.

22 THURSDAY ☿ *Moon Age Day 15* *Moon Sign Taurus*

A boost to teamwork and all co-operative ventures comes along at this time and you should make the most of these positive trends. You are getting on well with just about everyone, even if there are one or two awkward types around. Your creative potential is especially good and some Pisceans will be thinking about redecorating.

23 FRIDAY ☿ *Moon Age Day 16* *Moon Sign Taurus*

When it comes to furthering your ambitions you are clearly second to none, even though you might have to enlist the support of others on the way. There are likely to be some unexpected events around this time but you should manage to deal with them relatively easily. If you are currently single, there is a chance you could start a new relationship now.

24 SATURDAY ☿ *Moon Age Day 17* *Moon Sign Gemini*

Close companions may now cause you to think quite deeply about the importance you have placed upon relationships of late. It is possible that you may decide to spend some of your social hours with people you don't see very often. This would be a good day for sending letters or for making a long-distance telephone call.

25 SUNDAY ☿ *Moon Age Day 18   Moon Sign Gemini*

New life may now be breathed into situations you thought were over and done with. Expect friends to take you into their confidence, and make sure you understand the importance of keeping it. Friends are likely to be particularly demanding of your time and that won't leave quite as many hours as you might have wished for practical matters.

26 MONDAY ☿ *Moon Age Day 19   Moon Sign Cancer*

Self-confidence in professional matters is clearly the way forward and you won't get anywhere at all if you fail to show those around you that you know what you are talking about. In social and family situations you are putting everyone ahead of yourself, which isn't exactly unusual for Pisces.

27 TUESDAY ☿ *Moon Age Day 20   Moon Sign Cancer*

There may be a number of advantages for you in assuming a high profile in connection with your professional life. It doesn't matter how lowly you consider your position at work to be, you now have the ability to make it really count. For some Pisceans, there are new responsibilities on offer.

28 WEDNESDAY ☿ *Moon Age Day 21   Moon Sign Leo*

Long-term ambitions and major aims are likely to be within easier reach at this stage. Your future is now more definitely in your own hands than seems to have been the case for a while. The middle of the working week may also bring you to a specific decision that has been pending for ages. Friends should prove helpful now.

29 THURSDAY ☿ *Moon Age Day 22   Moon Sign Leo*

Your intuition is now much increased and you need to turn it in the direction of people who are coming new into your life. These might be individuals who you meet professionally, or perhaps potential friends for the future. Not everything is what it seems – and you have what it takes to work out why.

30 FRIDAY ☿ *Moon Age Day 23   Moon Sign Virgo*

You now have to put up with the lunar low, though for a host of astrological reasons you might fail to even notice its presence now. The fact is that you have great momentum and can shoot through difficult moments without registering them. You do have to watch out for the odd conman though, because not everyone is trustworthy.

December
2018

1 SATURDAY ☿ *Moon Age Day 24   Moon Sign Virgo*

A lack of progress could annoy you today although there is a good chance that you won't lose too much momentum, or else you are not really seeking any. Some Pisceans will be slowing down a little now, and as it is the weekend you can indulge any desire to enjoy yourself without any sense of guilt.

2 SUNDAY ☿ *Moon Age Day 25   Moon Sign Libra*

The things that are the most enjoyable now are to be found out there in the wider world. With plenty to play for and more than a modicum of good luck on your side, you can afford to back your hunches. People you haven't seen for some time could soon be in touch and correspondence generally proves important.

3 MONDAY ☿ *Moon Age Day 26   Moon Sign Libra*

The things you learn from colleagues today can be of supreme importance, so you must pay attention to what is said around you. Pisceans who are looking for work or a change of employment could also be in luck around this time. When it comes to out-of-work activities, new interests take your fancy.

4 TUESDAY ☿ *Moon Age Day 27   Moon Sign Scorpio*

The ideas that others have will not be exactly to your liking now and you are much more likely to focus on your own schemes and plans. Whether or not you can bring important people round to your way of thinking remains to be seen. There are some quite significant changes up ahead for some Pisceans.

5 WEDNESDAY ☿ *Moon Age Day 28* *Moon Sign Scorpio*

It is now the more practical aspects of life that appeal to you the most. In the main, you will want to do your own thing today and won't take kindly to being bossed around by anyone. The end of a particular phase in your life is not too far away and although it will bring the odd sigh of nostalgia, the gains outweigh the losses.

6 THURSDAY ☿ *Moon Age Day 29* *Moon Sign Scorpio*

You should enjoy being on the move as much as possible but don't allow distractions to get in the way of real financial success. Dragging yourself back to practicalities might not seem all that inspiring but could prove to be quite important all the same. It is also a good time to begin making plans for Christmas.

7 FRIDAY *Moon Age Day 0* *Moon Sign Sagittarius*

Don't dither or hang back when it comes to making major decisions. The more ambitious you are, the greater is the potential for success. Results you have been seeking for some time will be closer than you think and you have tremendous potential for doing just the right thing when it matters the most.

8 SATURDAY *Moon Age Day 1* *Moon Sign Sagittarius*

The planetary emphasis falls on finances, probably not surprising at this expensive time of the year. You are quite canny at the moment and know full well how to get value for money. Look around because there could be one or two things available for Christmas that you can get at rock-bottom prices.

9 SUNDAY *Moon Age Day 2* *Moon Sign Capricorn*

A possible mistake you might make today is to take on too many diverse interests. You would be much better off concentrating on one thing at a time and therefore avoiding unnecessary mistakes. Methodical actions may lead to success, but there will still be plenty of time in which to enjoy yourself.

10 MONDAY
Moon Age Day 3   Moon Sign Capricorn

A fast pace of events in the professional or practical world is probably what you can expect today. There is vital information there for the taking and you won't be slow to pick up on what others are trying to tell you. Give yourself a pat on the back for a recent personal success but don't allow it to go to your head.

11 TUESDAY
Moon Age Day 4   Moon Sign Aquarius

Faces old and new come along now ahead of the Christmas period. You might be deliberately taking a trip down memory lane at some stage today because that is what Christmas is all about. With less than two weeks to go, most Pisceans should now be pleased with the arrangements they have made for the holidays.

12 WEDNESDAY
Moon Age Day 5   Moon Sign Aquarius

A continuing improvement in a general sense makes itself felt most in terms of work and your ability to attract money. Your decision-making is good at present and you can afford to back your hunches to a greater extent. Friends should prove to be quite reliable and there are some new pals in the offing.

13 THURSDAY
Moon Age Day 6   Moon Sign Aquarius

A sense of variety and freedom is both important and appealing to Pisceans at this time. Don't be a stick-in-the-mud. Although this might not be exactly the season for outdoor activities, you might find the lure of the wild appealing. Later in the day, you might choose to spend at least some time alone.

14 FRIDAY
Moon Age Day 7   Moon Sign Pisces

Getting into heated debates could be more enjoyable than you might imagine and with the lunar high now present, you are hardly likely to lose. Back your hunches to the hilt and do what you can to make progress your middle name. There isn't too much time before the holidays, so make the best of what is available.

15 SATURDAY   *Moon Age Day 8   Moon Sign Pisces*

Your potential for lucky breaks is greater than usual and you won't be inclined to look on the dark side of any situation at present. Getting favours from others proves to be especially easy and your general level of popularity seems higher than ever. In reality, you are always popular but you realise it more at this time.

16 SUNDAY   *Moon Age Day 9   Moon Sign Pisces*

The quickening pace around you in everyday life shows at every turn and you will barely have time to breathe right now. Don't leave travel plans to chance but make sure that all details are sorted well in advance. This might be a journey you intend to take this week or perhaps even as late as Christmas or New Year.

17 MONDAY   *Moon Age Day 10   Moon Sign Aries*

A boost to all social matters comes along and it looks as though you are already well into a Christmas frame of mind. All is happiness around you and if you have been a little restricted by the negative attitude of friends or family members, this sort of situation is now likely to be disappearing.

18 TUESDAY   *Moon Age Day 11   Moon Sign Aries*

Intellectual inspiration comes your way via travel and social discussions. It seems that others find you extremely entertaining to have around and they could be making you feel almost like a celebrity at the moment. Expect friends to share confidences with you, even some friends who are not usually forthcoming with their problems.

19 WEDNESDAY   *Moon Age Day 12   Moon Sign Taurus*

Some people might describe you as being too assertive at present but if they do it's probably only because they are used to getting their own way. All that is happening is that you know what you want from life and are presently willing to say so. Avoid getting into pointless discussions about things that don't matter.

20 THURSDAY
Moon Age Day 13   Moon Sign Taurus

You can capitalise on new opportunities today and won't be stuck when it comes to expressing your opinions, no matter who is on the receiving end. Although you might not have too much professional influence for today, there are ideas coming into your mind at the moment that you will act upon before long.

21 FRIDAY
Moon Age Day 14   Moon Sign Gemini

You are presently filled with a definite urge to work hard and to get what you want from life. Not everyone is in the same frame of mind as you are and there isn't much doubt that people's general holiday spirit is getting in your way at a time when you are in a practical mood. Some Piscean patience is called for.

22 SATURDAY
Moon Age Day 15   Moon Sign Gemini

This can be an especially rewarding day for many Pisceans, a situation that is brought about as a result of a cocktail of positive planetary positions. You may be able to confirm one or two suspicions regarding someone you haven't trusted for a while but in the main you find others to be reliable and helpful.

23 SUNDAY
Moon Age Day 16   Moon Sign Cancer

This would be a good time to take a short break and to mull over your present successes. Of course you won't be able to see everything in its true light just at the moment but where it matters the most you begin to see some light at the end of the tunnel. Friends will demand your time but you will help if you can.

24 MONDAY
Moon Age Day 17   Moon Sign Cancer

Christmas Eve is likely to see an increase in general progress, followed by a lull that comes later in the day. Routines will be tedious, though it won't be long before the excitement of the day takes over. Family members are the source of much joy and you should be happily looking forward to tomorrow.

25 TUESDAY   *Moon Age Day 18   Moon Sign Leo*

Although you may feel a need to get out of doors to soak up the Christmas spirit, this won't stop you from having a particularly good and enjoyable day. Travel is most likely to come very soon but for the moment, enjoy feeling warm, secure and surrounded by love in the bosom of your family.

26 WEDNESDAY   *Moon Age Day 19   Moon Sign Leo*

Positive influences surround social gatherings, which probably makes Boxing Day the most potentially riotous and enjoyable day of the holidays. You are less inclined to seek your own surroundings now, so perhaps you are deciding to go on a family visit. Routine jobs should definitely be put on hold at present.

27 THURSDAY   *Moon Age Day 20   Moon Sign Virgo*

Some of the things that are happening around you now seem less fulfilling. You need to broaden your horizons somewhat and should not be intimidated by little setbacks. The lunar low doesn't really help the situation but whether or not you enjoy what today has on offer seems to be up to you.

28 FRIDAY   *Moon Age Day 21   Moon Sign Virgo*

Although you are in the middle of a planetary lull, you can still make the most of today. Let others make the running and simply turn up to have a good time. At least part of today will be spent deliberately alone, perhaps thinking about the year that lies ahead. A more positive attitude comes along by the evening.

29 SATURDAY   *Moon Age Day 22   Moon Sign Libra*

Right now you should be enjoying high points in love and romantic affairs, not to mention a definite boost to your ego that comes from a number of different directions. You clearly believe in yourself and while this is the case you won't be short of ideas or ways in which you can make them work out as you would wish.

30 SUNDAY
Moon Age Day 23   Moon Sign Libra

Stand by for a fairly brisk time socially and you will almost certainly find that some of the recent frustrations are now disappearing. Your confidence is strong but you are willing to suspend some actions until next week. As a result there is more time available to simply enjoy yourself in the company of family and friends.

31 MONDAY
Moon Age Day 24   Moon Sign Libra

It is just possible that your love life might unfortunately prove to be slightly problematic on this New Year's Eve. Although this reminds you that you have to show that extra bit of concern and love, take heart from the fact that it shouldn't be a lasting situation. If you open your eyes to the needs of those around you, it is possible to have everything fully on course for a splendid evening.

PISCES:
2019 DIARY PAGES

PISCES:
YOUR YEAR IN BRIEF

Your year gets off to an interesting start. You are surer of yourself than usual, which could come as a surprise to quite a few people. Both January and February offer new and fascinating diversions and both months should also be better than average when it comes to romance. Exercise a little caution regarding money and save what you can because you could travel more during the coming year than you sometimes might.

March and April might be slightly quieter months but still offer a great deal in the way of opportunities. This time could see you making headway as a result of your previous hard work and, what's more, people begin to recognise your potential. People from the past now begin to exert a strong influence in your life, whilst at the same time new friends and associates also count.

In May and June you should find yourself in the right mood for travel and for diversity. You certainly won't take kindly to being restricted or kept doing the same tasks all the time and if this has been the case in your career, you could now be looking for new challenges. Your love life should be good and as the weather begins to warm up, so do your passions. Look out for new people in your life who bring a wind of change with them.

July and August see you at your liveliest and best. There are times when you will need to check and recheck certain details, but that's simply so you can get the very best out of any given situation. You won't worry if you are put in charge of almost anything and may even discover talents that you didn't know you had.

Look forward to September and October because they will probably turn out to be the two most significant months of the year. Money is an issue that looks particularly good at this time and there might be more to spend and to save than you had been anticipating. Don't expect miracles, of course, but make the most of your ability to address issues, to take command and to show people what you are worth – and financial reward may be the natural consequence.

November and December should be settled, happy and in the main successful. You end the year with surplus energy and with new opportunities surrounding you on all sides. You might need to watch what you are spending during December but personal gains more than compensate for any temporary financial shortfall. Christmas should be particularly memorable and eventful this time around and there will be no doubting your popularity or your personal magnetism. Your sense of fun will be limitless as the year ends.

January
2019

1 TUESDAY
Moon Age Day 25   Moon Sign Scorpio

Your ability to win friends and influence people is noteworthy on this New Year's Day so don't miss any opportunity that comes along to get what you need or want. You start the year feeling confident and the sometimes slightly retiring qualities of Pisces don't seem to be on display now.

2 WEDNESDAY
Moon Age Day 26   Moon Sign Scorpio

Look for a change of scenery if you really want to keep smiling today. You won't want to be stuck in the same place and diversity is what really fires off your imagination under present trends. Mental and intellectual matters are uppermost in your thoughts and you would be incredible at solving puzzles now.

3 THURSDAY
Moon Age Day 27   Moon Sign Sagittarius

Information coming your way from a friend or associate could do much to brighten your day. Your state of mind generally can be improved as a result of social possibilities that are coming your way now. Romance also cannot be ruled out as being an important component of this period.

4 FRIDAY
Moon Age Day 28   Moon Sign Sagittarius

You might have to learn to use a little more concentration when it comes to assessing the needs of those around you. This is an unusual statement to make to anyone born under the zodiac sign of Pisces, which is the most caring sign of them all. However, for today the position of the Moon is doing you few favours.

73

5 SATURDAY
Moon Age Day 0   Moon Sign Capricorn

New input should be welcomed with open arms around this time. This is a great time for making new contacts, whether these are people you seek for yourself or not. Everyone seems to want to be your friend at the moment so there is no reason to feel quite as nervous about situations as you sometimes do.

6 SUNDAY
Moon Age Day 1   Moon Sign Capricorn

There are now exciting social possibilities to consider, although not for long because today you really need to act quickly. You can have a really good time in the company of people who have a very casual attitude to life. Sometimes this is good for a person who is generally a very deep thinker.

7 MONDAY
Moon Age Day 2   Moon Sign Capricorn

Social invitations are likely to come thick and fast now and they bring with them the chance to really enjoy what the start of the working week has to offer. If you have been looking for love, it is quite possible you will find it under present trends. Don't give in if there is something you really want.

8 TUESDAY
Moon Age Day 3   Moon Sign Aquarius

Avoid unnecessary assumptions and bear in mind that you could be rather susceptible to deception, or prone to fall for hidden schemes around now. This would not be a good time to sign any documents unless you are sure of the small print. Confidences from friends must be strictly kept at this time.

9 WEDNESDAY
Moon Age Day 4   Moon Sign Aquarius

You really do need to get your act together in a professional sense if you want to take full advantage of an offer that is about to come your way. It's possible that you will doubt yourself, which is a pity because you seem to be on top form and will excel in situations that puzzle those around you.

10 THURSDAY   *Moon Age Day 5   Moon Sign Pisces*

The lunar high brings many favours and high spots into your life. When it comes to making fresh starts you could hardly be doing better and all the planning you did yesterday now begins to pay off. Expect a noticeable boost in both professional and social matters.

11 FRIDAY   *Moon Age Day 6   Moon Sign Pisces*

Now your personal horizons will broaden immeasurably. You believe in yourself and that's worth so much. Romance is particularly well highlighted, not only by the lunar high but also by other planetary positions in your chart. In a practical or a professional sense it is very important to strike while the iron is hot.

12 SATURDAY   *Moon Age Day 7   Moon Sign Pisces*

Today should have a very good feel to it. Be on the lookout for old faces but also enjoy the social possibilities that come thanks to new friends. Keep a sense of proportion if you feel worried in social gatherings and understand that you are making a much better impression than you realise.

13 SUNDAY   *Moon Age Day 8   Moon Sign Aries*

Don't believe everything you hear from others at the moment and then you won't be too disappointed when things don't go the way you might have wished. If you have wisely put a reserve plan in place you should use it now. Prepare to have to deal with something or someone tricky.

14 MONDAY   *Moon Age Day 9   Moon Sign Aries*

You should still be wary about being led up the garden path by others today but since your intuition seems to serve you well, this is far less likely than might have been the case even yesterday. You prefer to proceed under your own steam for the moment and that's fine. Don't allow anyone to push you.

15 TUESDAY *Moon Age Day 10   Moon Sign Taurus*

At this time your thoughts on your love life could give you cause to stop and think. Let your partner know what's on your mind and if you don't have a partner, rely on the help and advice of a good friend. At least some family matters might be put on hold for the moment to allow you some breathing space.

16 WEDNESDAY *Moon Age Day 11   Moon Sign Taurus*

A gradual shift to a better financial position seems possible, starting today. You are wise in your judgements and won't be taking unnecessary chances. At the same time you know a bargain when you see one and should be in a good position to add to small amounts of cash that are likely to come your way.

17 THURSDAY *Moon Age Day 12   Moon Sign Taurus*

Today's trends mean you are likely to be looking for convivial surroundings and an easy-going atmosphere. You won't want to sort out the arguments of others and nor would you presently be willing to dump your own ideas at the whim of friends. Taken all in all, Pisces can be awkward now, but understandably so.

18 FRIDAY *Moon Age Day 13   Moon Sign Gemini*

While your mind might be working overtime at the moment, it's all you can do to keep up physically. Lacking in the planetary support that brings physical energy, you will probably tire more easily than usual. There are ways round everything, though. Perhaps allow your friends to take some of the strain?

19 SATURDAY *Moon Age Day 14   Moon Sign Gemini*

Social invitations are now likely to come in thick and fast, making for an excellent weekend for many Pisceans. There are times when you won't wait to be asked but will be making the running yourself. Someone is going to be very surprised when they see you pushing yourself forward in this way.

20 SUNDAY *Moon Age Day 15   Moon Sign Cancer*

You will want to keep up a varied social life and there is just a possibility that other responsibilities might get in the way of you doing so, especially if you work at the weekend. Look towards a particular objective because every small step you take in the right direction helps to lead you to your ultimate goal.

21 MONDAY *Moon Age Day 16   Moon Sign Cancer*

This is not the time to be tempting fate with risky ventures. At the same time you could have just a little trouble in expressing yourself in the way you would wish. Instead of trying to push ahead today, take some time out to think about life and to watch others accomplishing things.

22 TUESDAY *Moon Age Day 17   Moon Sign Leo*

Things change and a great deal of enthusiasm is now likely to go into communication and social interactions today. You have what it takes to be the centre of attention and that can be of particular help to you in a professional sense. This is the time to dust off a few of your more grandiose ideas and to introduce them to the world.

23 WEDNESDAY *Moon Age Day 18   Moon Sign Leo*

This is a wonderful time for friendships and for getting people on your side. The naturally charming side of your nature is shining out like a beacon and practically everyone wants to be your friend. It is difficult to dislike Pisceans and with the way you are behaving at the moment it is almost impossible.

24 THURSDAY *Moon Age Day 19   Moon Sign Virgo*

It might feel as though certain aspects of your life are at a standstill but this is only the lunar low holding you back a little. Your confidence is low but you can get things moving by accepting that the Moon only stays in your opposite sign for a very short period. Plan and look ahead, whilst staying optimistic.

25 FRIDAY
Moon Age Day 20   Moon Sign Virgo

This is a planetary low spot and a time during which everyone around you seems to be making more progress than you are. Remain patient and concentrate on things that are not dependant on your personal effort. Working with others might help, if you allow them to make most of the decisions.

26 SATURDAY
Moon Age Day 21   Moon Sign Libra

If you are uncertain today about your goals and objectives, take some time out. Pisces always needs quiet interludes and a good deal of meditation. Today works better if you take life one step at a time and if you avoid getting involved in situations you either don't understand or simply dislike.

27 SUNDAY
Moon Age Day 22   Moon Sign Libra

The trends are favourable for social ambitions this Sunday and all group activities are especially well highlighted under present planetary trends. You are able to offer significant help and support to those who need it. Even if you don't know the people concerned you have what it takes to lend a hand.

28 MONDAY
Moon Age Day 23   Moon Sign Scorpio

You now have a quite unworldly angle on personal matters, which is characterised by selflessness and high ideals. That's fine, but the world won't always match up to your expectations of it. You can't help being the sort of person you are, but your natural sensitivity can sometimes lead to disappointment.

29 TUESDAY
Moon Age Day 24   Moon Sign Scorpio

Communications at this time may involve tension or ego on the part of others. Adapting yourself to this state of affairs isn't difficult but it might become tiring having to play a defensive role. The answer is simple – take yourself away from the offending people for an hour or two and do something that pleases you.

30 WEDNESDAY *Moon Age Day 25 Moon Sign Sagittarius*

You need to keep a strong element of variety in your life now and shouldn't be too willing to stick to the same old midweek routines. Not only do you please yourself by bringing a little change into your day, but others will be happy too. Not everyone you meet is going to be pleasant but don't worry – that's life.

31 THURSDAY *Moon Age Day 26 Moon Sign Sagittarius*

Compassion is your middle name, especially so today. By helping others, you invariably do yourself some good too, though of course that is not why you offer assistance. Modest and unassuming, you should find a groundswell of affection coming at you from most of the people you meet today.

February

2019

1 FRIDAY
Moon Age Day 27   Moon Sign Sagittarius

Recent small successes could prove to be much more, just as long as you concentrate and don't allow others to make either the running or the decisions. You are very astute at present and you have a strong instinct for what is the right action in any given situation. As a result, your level of confidence grows.

2 SATURDAY
Moon Age Day 28   Moon Sign Capricorn

You should enjoy the cut and thrust of relationships immensely this weekend and can gain a great deal, simply from being around people you recognise as being successful in their own right. You might detect a small but steadily growing desire to break out of some social or personal constraints.

3 SUNDAY
Moon Age Day 29   Moon Sign Capricorn

You may need to assume a more dominant role in your family but this may well turn out to be a very good thing. Although it could seem to you that you are lording it over others, nothing could be further from the truth. Partnerships of all sorts are well highlighted under present planetary trends.

4 MONDAY
Moon Age Day 0   Moon Sign Aquarius

The emphasis now shifts to social fun and you should have little or no trouble finding yourself in precisely the right company at just the right time. There are quieter moments too, because the Moon is entering your solar twelfth house but in the main you are out for a good time, most likely with friends.

5 TUESDAY   *Moon Age Day 1   Moon Sign Aquarius*

You won't lack stamina now and can achieve a good deal, simply by bulldozing your way through situations. Maybe you will not show the same degree of sensitivity as is usually the case but you can make rapid progress in a number of different areas. If your memory lets you down it is probably because you are overloading it.

6 WEDNESDAY   *Moon Age Day 2   Moon Sign Aquarius*

If there are any frustrations about today, they are likely to come about as a result of the activities of others. Unfortunately, you will have to take these in your stride because there is very little you can do about them. A mixture of loyalty and Piscean sensitivity are likely to prevent you from firing back.

7 THURSDAY   *Moon Age Day 3   Moon Sign Pisces*

The Moon returns to your zodiac sign, offering an excellent day, with plenty to set it apart and no lack of attention coming your way. Now might be the time to take a small chance financially because good luck is likely to be with you. Conforming to expectations might be hard but you should manage it now.

8 FRIDAY   *Moon Age Day 4   Moon Sign Pisces*

This Friday is a very positive one indeed. You should be feeling on top form, your intellect is razor sharp and you are very funny. People actively want to have you around and you might even discover some social options you hadn't thought of previously. Don't be surprised if you are being treated as number one.

9 SATURDAY   *Moon Age Day 5   Moon Sign Aries*

This should continue to be a positive period on the domestic scene. It looks as though you are in for some interesting times with regard to family members, with younger people figuring strongly. Although you won't consider yourself to be particularly lucky at the moment, some gains are possible.

10 SUNDAY *Moon Age Day 6   Moon Sign Aries*

It looks as though you will be in the best of company at the moment. With newer and better invitations leading you down some unfamiliar paths, you will need to be on the ball today. Although you can sometimes be slightly shy in unfamiliar setting, this isn't likely to be the case right now.

11 MONDAY *Moon Age Day 7   Moon Sign Aries*

You are especially sensitive to the feelings of those around you as this new week gets underway. Although you want to please everyone, this won't be possible and it will almost certainly be necessary for you to speak your mind at some stage. Where finances are concerned, hold on tight to money for the moment.

12 TUESDAY *Moon Age Day 8   Moon Sign Taurus*

It is quite likely you will be thinking about personal issues today and perhaps seeking to change the ground rules with regard to a relationship. People you haven't seen for some time could come back into your life, bringing with them some surprising news.

13 WEDNESDAY *Moon Age Day 9   Moon Sign Taurus*

Moneymaking endeavours are well-starred and continue to be so between now and the weekend. Although you won't want to take too many chances, you do have a kind of astrological guardian angel looking over you. When it comes to putting forward your unique point of view, tell it how it is.

14 THURSDAY *Moon Age Day 10   Moon Sign Gemini*

Any opportunity to make new and influential business contacts should not be passed by. This is especially true if you are self-employed or in a management position. Offers that are made outside of work may well include social gatherings that you find fascinating. Don't allow shyness to hold you back.

15 FRIDAY   *Moon Age Day 11   Moon Sign Gemini*

When it comes to dealing with others, there are now a few obstacles to deal with. Not everyone is behaving in quite the way you would expect and you are perhaps a little touchy at present. There could be occasions today when you will need to exercise that famous Piscean patience, though it won't be easy.

16 SATURDAY   *Moon Age Day 12   Moon Sign Cancer*

This may prove to be a very busy period at home and a time during which you are offering a good deal of support to loved ones. As far as the practicalities of life are concerned, you should be able to address these with very little trouble. Getting on-side with colleagues might bring one or two small problems.

17 SUNDAY   *Moon Age Day 13   Moon Sign Cancer*

Though the emotional influences surrounding you at the moment are not in any way heavy, you are still too sensitive in some ways. Try to keep it light and breezy today and to mix as freely as you can with the sort of people who fire your imagination and your sense of fun.

18 MONDAY   *Moon Age Day 14   Moon Sign Leo*

Where work is concerned it is clear that you will have to pace yourself today, and this doesn't simply apply to your professional life. When it comes to getting chores done around the house you will want to take your time but you can also sort things out much better if you enlist a little practical help.

19 TUESDAY   *Moon Age Day 15   Moon Sign Leo*

Strong feelings have a large role to play between yourself and someone else – most probably at work. You should certainly be feeling quite sure of something. Don't become agitated if things don't always seem to go your way. Your social prospects are also good now so perhaps get out this evening?

20 WEDNESDAY   *Moon Age Day 16   Moon Sign Virgo*

Things could now slow down somewhat for two reasons. First, the lunar low is around; secondly, the sort of progress you have been making is tied to practical and professional matters, which are not well-starred. Although you may feel impatient, try to show the quieter and more reflective face of Pisces.

21 THURSDAY   *Moon Age Day 17   Moon Sign Virgo*

This is a time to catch up with intimate relationships and to stay mainly in the bosom of your family. Nobody is forcing you down this road and, in any case, the temporary respite will prove to have been extremely useful once tomorrow comes. At the back of your mind there is a good deal of planning and scheming taking place.

22 FRIDAY   *Moon Age Day 18   Moon Sign Libra*

A period of significant optimism now begins. The Sun is entering your solar first house, where it remains for the next month or so. It should be much easier to make life work the way you would wish, whilst at the same time you will notice just how much more responsive other people seem to be.

23 SATURDAY   *Moon Age Day 19   Moon Sign Libra*

You seem to dominate your domestic surroundings at present, which is probably no bad thing now that the weekend has arrived. The difficulties that might come into the lives of those you love are dealt with efficiently by your typical Piscean temperament. Trends suggest that your partner may be in a very strange frame of mind.

24 SUNDAY   *Moon Age Day 20   Moon Sign Scorpio*

There is great potential for new friendships to start at any time now. Pisces generally keeps its friends, often for life, but you do need new stimulus now and again and that is what is on offer at present. Don't turn down the chance for an exciting encounter with someone you hold in high regard.

25 MONDAY   *Moon Age Day 21   Moon Sign Scorpio*

Try to avoid manipulating others at home, whilst at the same time keeping an eye on them. It's a fine line to walk but if anyone can achieve it, you can. Don't get involved in power games, either at work or at home. You have your own way of getting to where you need to be and you are not a pushy type.

26 TUESDAY   *Moon Age Day 22   Moon Sign Sagittarius*

Just the right type of influences are present today and they come courtesy of one of the best planetary line-ups for ages as far as you are concerned. Your intuition is especially strong and won't let you down when it comes to making decisions. Your personal life should also be taking a turn for the better.

27 WEDNESDAY   *Moon Age Day 23   Moon Sign Sagittarius*

There is likely to be some turmoil in your life today, but it is more than matched by your ability to deal with matters as and when they come along. Too much prior planning may be difficult, if not impossible, so you need to keep your eye on the ball. Personal relationships should seem stronger as the day unfolds.

28 THURSDAY   *Moon Age Day 24   Moon Sign Sagittarius*

You should be confident and possibly achieving a physical peak in terms of energy today. With everything to play for, this is likely to be a day to remember. When it comes to the influence you have over others, you seem to be on especially good form, so now is the time to ask for what you really want.

March

2019

1 FRIDAY
Moon Age Day 25   Moon Sign Capricorn

The sort of fun you are seeking today might be unavailable but that doesn't mean you shouldn't look for it. In fact, you may be able to pep things up yourself and it looks as though you have what it takes to make an impression. Pisces is a very understated sign, which is why you are so obvious when you do turn up the volume.

2 SATURDAY
Moon Age Day 26   Moon Sign Capricorn

Partnerships improve and it doesn't matter if these are of a professional or a personal nature. Almost anyone can be of use to you at the moment and it is clear that your mixture of intuition and practical common sense is what is leading you forward. Expect to hear some messages from people you don't see very often.

3 SUNDAY
Moon Age Day 27   Moon Sign Aquarius

A helping hand can be quite important to you at this time and offers you the chance to get ahead in something you didn't really think you were good at. Seek out those who are in the know and if you are deciding on some new sort of hobby, make sure everything is in place before you get started. It's vital to do so.

4 MONDAY
Moon Age Day 28   Moon Sign Aquarius

Whenever you are working amongst groups around this time you find you can shine like a bright star. It isn't that you leap to the front, determined to be the best of the bunch, but rather your great co-operation and team spirit that matter. At work you could find rules and regulations to be a drag.

5 TUESDAY　　　*Moon Age Day 29　Moon Sign Aquarius*

You should steam ahead with most of your ambitions today, particularly if red tape at work slowed you down yesterday. Your chart now indicates a very promising high spot in your romantic life. Whether you have a settled relationship or not, you won't be able to deny that you feel happy and secure.

6 WEDNESDAY　☿　*Moon Age Day 0　Moon Sign Pisces*

You should be preparing to put new initiatives into action and there isn't much doubt about your ability to get ahead in a very positive way. The lunar high is the icing on the cake today and adds to a wealth of good planetary positions that are around you now. Your creative potential is also especially good.

7 THURSDAY　☿　*Moon Age Day 1　Moon Sign Pisces*

This may turn out to be the luckiest day of the month but don't push things because you don't need to. Ease into the day as if you were driving a very powerful car around a fast track. You have all the skill you need to get to the finishing line. You are particularly good in professional matters today.

8 FRIDAY　☿　*Moon Age Day 2　Moon Sign Aries*

Excellent influences surround love and marriage, so it looks like today is a time when you will be turning to the one you love the most. They, in turn, will show their affection for you, maybe even in very practical ways. Trends also suggest that you may receive some unexpected benefits.

9 SATURDAY　☿　*Moon Age Day 3　Moon Sign Aries*

Money-wise you should discover that things are coming together even better than you expected. Of course this depends whether or not you even choose to look at such matters today. Certainly there is plenty else that could occupy your mind and you won't be stuck for exciting ways to have a good time.

10 SUNDAY ☿ *Moon Age Day 4   Moon Sign Taurus*

This could turn out to be an emotionally tense time and a period during which you will have to look at things in a logical way. This isn't always easy for Pisces but it is possible that you are likely to jump to the wrong conclusions otherwise. If you are in doubt about anything, ask someone you consider to be wise.

11 MONDAY ☿ *Moon Age Day 5   Moon Sign Taurus*

Something very exciting may come along today. Perhaps it's a project you started some time ago or it might just be that you are anxious to get ahead generally. Whatever you undertake, you can now do it with vigour. There are gains to be made at work, or maybe a new job in the pipeline if you are between positions.

12 TUESDAY ☿ *Moon Age Day 6   Moon Sign Taurus*

Press ahead with important plans and allow others to do what comes naturally to them. You are inclined to work alongside those you care for, either as friends or relatives, but you can't live their lives for them. In any case, there are times when Pisces needs to think and act in isolation. This is such a period.

13 WEDNESDAY ☿ *Moon Age Day 7   Moon Sign Gemini*

You may tend to let others overshadow you today but it is plain that you know what you are doing. The truth is that you sometimes deliberately take a back seat because that's the way you get others on your side. Pisces needs to be loved and always being at the top of the tree is a place you find too lonely.

14 THURSDAY ☿ *Moon Age Day 8   Moon Sign Gemini*

This would be a good time to surround yourself with friends. The aspects that lead to personal and professional success are not so numerous right now and so a degree of rest would be sensible. If you want to bask in the glory of things you have been doing up to now, then why not? Your popularity isn't in doubt.

15 FRIDAY ☿ *Moon Age Day 9   Moon Sign Cancer*

The main emphasis for today seems to be on family matters and the way you deal with them is quite important. Younger people in particular could be giving you the odd problem but yours is a very understanding zodiac sign and that shows now. At work you should be anxious to make a good impression.

16 SATURDAY ☿ *Moon Age Day 10   Moon Sign Cancer*

It should not be difficult to attract the good things in life this weekend and for once you recognise the value of a little luxury in your life. If someone wants to make a fuss of you, it might be churlish to refuse their kindness. In an artistic sense you show good judgement today so perhaps it might be a good time to buy a new picture for your home.

17 SUNDAY ☿ *Moon Age Day 11   Moon Sign Cancer*

The Sun remains in your solar first house, bringing energy and confidence in the main. Although you have what it takes to get ahead, you might be held up because of your constant concern for others. Try to offload just a few of your responsibilities, many of which are not yours in the first place.

18 MONDAY ☿ *Moon Age Day 12   Moon Sign Leo*

Though family needs are once again likely to take priority today, you will have time to mix with your friends, which is quite important at the moment. Be careful that you don't step on the toes of someone who has real influence in your professional life. Your usual diplomatic approach to situations now works best.

19 TUESDAY ☿ *Moon Age Day 13   Moon Sign Leo*

Avoid being heavy-handed in your dealings with family members. It might be best to stay away from family issues for the moment, in favour of spending as much time as you can amongst friends. Not everyone to whom you are related is on the same wavelength as you are right now and that's where the problems start.

20 WEDNESDAY ☿ *Moon Age Day 14 Moon Sign Virgo*

Close a few operations down today and plan new ones. Your strategy so far this month has been great and there isn't much doubt about the positive impression you are making on those around you. What a good day this would be to cuddle up and enjoy the company of the one you care for the most.

21 THURSDAY ☿ *Moon Age Day 15 Moon Sign Virgo*

This looks like the right time to take your foot off the gas and to coast for a while. You need to take stock and if you are aware that this is the case, the lunar low will have very little negative impact on your life as a whole. Even apparently casual conversations can be worth a great deal today.

22 FRIDAY ☿ *Moon Age Day 16 Moon Sign Libra*

Your sense of self-determination has rarely looked better than it does at the moment. Most Pisceans will now be very single-minded and few people will argue with your point of view when they recognise the power you are generating. You don't have to shout at anyone to get what you want at present – a simple look should do.

23 SATURDAY ☿ *Moon Age Day 17 Moon Sign Libra*

As the Sun is about to leave your solar first house, you need to take the final step today towards an objective that is very important to you. You can get ahead quite easily, especially if you are at work. It isn't out of the question that advancement of some sort will be on offer before today is out.

24 SUNDAY ☿ *Moon Age Day 18 Moon Sign Scorpio*

You can win friends and influence people with very little effort at the moment. Pisces is at its influential best and you only have to speak to get what you want. This is fine but doesn't answer the more personal questions you are asking yourself at present. It might be time for a heart-to-heart with someone who is very important to you.

25 MONDAY   ☿   *Moon Age Day 19*   *Moon Sign Scorpio*

Make the best use of financial advantages that come your way around this time. Trust your intuition when dealing with others and offer the sort of advice that Pisceans find easy to give. Your concern for others is one of the reasons that so much attention now comes back in your direction.

26 TUESDAY   ☿ *Moon Age Day 20*   *Moon Sign Sagittarius*

Original ideas and insights today can advance your plans no end so you need to listen carefully to that little voice inside your head. You can get useful feedback from colleagues and friends, whilst at the same time responding to that very strong intuition. Almost everything is in the balance today.

27 WEDNESDAY ☿ *Moon Age Day 21*   *Moon Sign Sagittarius*

Emotions may run high today and this is probably one of the best days of the month when it comes to personal relationships. Finding the right words to tell someone how important they are to you will not be difficult and this is a day during which you could receive some unexpected but exciting invitations.

28 THURSDAY   ☿ *Moon Age Day 22*   *Moon Sign Capricorn*

You appear to have romantic expectations of today and will want to sweep your partner off their feet in some way. In your dealings with people in general, there is a danger that you could be rather too sensitive for your own good and may need to toughen up a little if you don't want to face a disappointment.

29 FRIDAY   *Moon Age Day 23*   *Moon Sign Capricorn*

You probably won't get your own way as much today as you would wish and may have to forego certain pleasures that you usually take for granted. Routines can be a bit of a bore and it is worth putting extra energy into jobs now so that they don't come back to haunt you later. Stopgap measures won't do.

30 SATURDAY · _Moon Age Day 24 · Moon Sign Capricorn_

Matters of love and affection are presently tempered by practical considerations. You must respond to some of the more practical matters that demand your attention and that means having to shelve your personal feelings just a little. You should find time later in the day to redress the balance a little.

31 SUNDAY · _Moon Age Day 25 · Moon Sign Aquarius_

In discussions of any sort you should be able to express yourself well. This doesn't mean you are browbeating anyone, simply that the magnetic quality of your personality is extremely strong. This would also be a good period for travel or for indulging a cultural interest that takes your fancy.

April
2019

1 MONDAY
Moon Age Day 26   Moon Sign Aquarius

This is a period during which intimate and private matters should be a source of emotional fulfilment, always an important factor in the life of a Piscean. There could be reasons to celebrate as a result of events within the family and you will be the first one to put out the flags.

2 TUESDAY
Moon Age Day 27   Moon Sign Pisces

You have all the support you require today with which to push your ideas forward. Any tendency to retreat into your own little world now disappears and you find yourself happy to be in the social flow and taking your place in the world. The lunar high should also bestow a greater degree of luck.

3 WEDNESDAY
Moon Age Day 28   Moon Sign Pisces

You easily outwit the competition as you take on new projects and are able to see all too clearly the nature of the path that lies before you. On the personal front, the number of compliments coming in at the moment bolsters your confidence and makes you able to react in a positive and even assertive way.

4 THURSDAY
Moon Age Day 29   Moon Sign Pisces

You can easily achieve any reasonable objectives you set yourself today, though you could also be inclined to retreat into yourself if you feel threatened in any way. By far the best response to any slight difficulties would be to face them squarely but this course of action won't be too easy for the moment.

5 FRIDAY
Moon Age Day 0   Moon Sign Aries

You have a pronounced tendency to be critical today. Fortunately, you exercise this quality only when you are faced with important decisions. The fact that you do not go blindly into any situation means you are simply being discriminating. This is especially important in terms of financial commitments.

6 SATURDAY
Moon Age Day 1   Moon Sign Aries

Everyday routine matters may be upset by unexpected events. If you remain flexible from the start, such eventualities will not cause too much in the way of concern. All the same, you can't expect everything to go smoothly at present and might have to rely on a little help from outside.

7 SUNDAY
Moon Age Day 2   Moon Sign Taurus

Your practical skills are well emphasised at this time. It is possible there are jobs around the house that you will want to undertake yourself, even if you have never tackled them before. With increasing belief in your ability and some positive support from someone close, now is the time to get stuck in.

8 MONDAY
Moon Age Day 3   Moon Sign Taurus

What matters for today is your versatility. People are turning to you for help and advice of a sort they feel only you can offer. The start of this week may be good from a financial point of view, particularly as a result of actions you took some time ago which are only now bearing fruit.

9 TUESDAY
Moon Age Day 4   Moon Sign Gemini

Expect to have to deal with some strong emotions today, though few of them are likely to be exhibited by you. It seems as though everyone has a unique and somewhat awkward point of view, which itself could lead to some disagreements. As usual, you will be expected to play the mediator.

10 WEDNESDAY   *Moon Age Day 5   Moon Sign Gemini*

You can be quite demanding in the personality stakes today, which isn't at all the normal state of affairs for Pisces. In addition, you are willing to push your way to the front of any queue and might even show yourself as being a little bossy. None of this is a problem but it could surprise a few people.

11 THURSDAY   *Moon Age Day 6   Moon Sign Gemini*

It is time to get down to business and to look very carefully at the practical side of life. You clearly have your thinking head on at the moment and will be easily able to deal with problems that are stumping others. Romance shows itself around this time, though it remains to be seen whether you have the time to notice it.

12 FRIDAY   *Moon Age Day 7   Moon Sign Cancer*

Personal and intimate subject matter brings out the best in you today. It is likely that you will be able to enjoy the support of loved ones, together with special friends in whom you put a high degree of trust. Committing yourself to new projects might not be all that easy today but should prove simpler tomorrow.

13 SATURDAY   *Moon Age Day 8   Moon Sign Cancer*

You can get the best from both worlds now. The domestic area of your life is likely to be very fulfilling but you can also make significant progress at work. If you have the chance to embark on a journey soon, perhaps a long one, you have the means at your disposal to broaden your horizons.

14 SUNDAY   *Moon Age Day 9   Moon Sign Leo*

Despite the fact that you keenly feel a number of obligations bearing down on you, today is good for all intellectual pursuits. Your mind is crystal clear and you can get through or around a number of potential obstacles. On the way, you are stretching yourself, which has to be a good thing under present trends.

15 MONDAY $\qquad$ *Moon Age Day 10   Moon Sign Leo*

Social and co-operative matters are positively highlighted and much of the joy you experience today comes through what you can do on behalf of others. This is fairly typical of the sign of Pisces and brings a fulfilling period, during which you feel a sense of rightness and balance.

16 TUESDAY $\qquad$ *Moon Age Day 11   Moon Sign Virgo*

Getting your own way in a monetary sense could turn out to be easier than you had expected. Simply turn on the charm, put forward a good, reasoned case and wait for the result. A degree of frugality may be necessary in the short-term, if only to prove to others you can practically live on fresh air. The lunar low makes this easy.

17 WEDNESDAY $\qquad$ *Moon Age Day 12   Moon Sign Virgo*

It would be a good idea to play safe in professional matters and to defer to the wisdom of people who know more about certain facts than you do. Worrying about your own limitations isn't wise though because you will lose some of the confidence you have in yourself at the moment.

18 THURSDAY $\qquad$ *Moon Age Day 13   Moon Sign Libra*

You might have to re-evaluate your attitude towards something in the domestic arena, though home life generally more than compensates for any lack of achievements in other areas of your life as this week rolls on. Younger family members in particular are likely to be a cause of joy.

19 FRIDAY $\qquad$ *Moon Age Day 14   Moon Sign Libra*

Domestic matters are now prone to a few disruptions but these are unlikely to bother you unduly. The problem, if it can be called that, is brought about by the present position of the Moon. You should avoid getting bogged down by pointless discussions or changes in your routines that prove unhelpful.

20 SATURDAY   *Moon Age Day 15   Moon Sign Scorpio*

You should feel happy to be useful today and will be of particular help to both family members and friends. You might not feel inclined to do a lot in the way of work but there are advantages to relaxing at the moment. Social trends look especially good and particularly so in the evening.

21 SUNDAY   *Moon Age Day 16   Moon Sign Scorpio*

Progress could be decidedly difficult to achieve, but you need to tell yourself that you cannot be pushing ahead all the time. Take stock of some situations and clear the decks for actions you know are going to come soon. Try to get some rest and, if possible, get involved in new hobbies or pastimes.

22 MONDAY   *Moon Age Day 17   Moon Sign Sagittarius*

A new idea that you put to the test today could turn out to be far more advantageous than you might think. This is likely to be one of your better days as far as financial progress is concerned and you should also be less likely to run into the buffers in personal matters. Things now look a good deal more optimistic.

23 TUESDAY   *Moon Age Day 18   Moon Sign Sagittarius*

Though career matters are likely to keep you very busy at this stage of the working week, you also need to find time to look after the interests of those you love. Your partner might be going through a few problems, whilst younger family members especially can gain a great deal from your experience.

24 WEDNESDAY   *Moon Age Day 19   Moon Sign Capricorn*

This is likely to be a rather pleasant period during which you are able to bring out the best in almost everyone you meet. Your intuition is as strong as ever and you might find that you are exceptionally curious about the way things work. A little investigation seems to be on the cards and could yield some unusual results.

25 THURSDAY *Moon Age Day 20   Moon Sign Capricorn*

Romance looks good now, though you approach it in a quiet way and won't want to ruffle any feathers by showing your affection for more than one person. You are able to stand and look at life as if it were a movie projected just for you, a fact that gives you a unique and useful perspective.

26 FRIDAY *Moon Age Day 21   Moon Sign Capricorn*

You should find that positive responses come from most people today and that is partly because of your own present attitude to life. Meetings with strangers could turn out to be very surprising indeed and might offer you new incentives you hadn't even thought about. Stand by for one of the most eventful periods of the month.

27 SATURDAY *Moon Age Day 22   Moon Sign Aquarius*

You should discover that most people do want to be in your good books at present and this can be of great assistance over this weekend. Social encounters are likely to turn out very pleasantly indeed, as will current issues associated with love. Make the weekend your own by being willing to take the lead.

28 SUNDAY *Moon Age Day 23   Moon Sign Aquarius*

This would be an ideal time to put new ideas to the test. It should not be difficult to get your own way in important negotiations, especially if they include other family members. The romantic side of Pisces is quite clearly on display so you will be strengthening attachments all round.

29 MONDAY *Moon Age Day 24   Moon Sign Pisces*

The planets may bring an effervescent quality to communications and you will be making a powerful impact on the big wide world. The lunar high coincides with a Monday, so you might be using most of that energy at work but you will want to do as much as you can to enliven your social life, too.

30 TUESDAY
Moon Age Day 25   Moon Sign Pisces

Your spirits are likely to be extremely high today and there is no better way to start a spring Tuesday than with the Moon in your own zodiac sign. Don't take no for an answer when you are certain of your position and be willing to take a few calculated risks in order to get exactly what you want from life.

May

2019

1 WEDNESDAY
Moon Age Day 26   Moon Sign Pisces

Optimism is strong today and there isn't much at which you will fail when you also have confidence in your own abilities. People notice the new you and are anxious to back a winner. That increases your popularity and might mean a good deal of attention coming your way during today.

2 THURSDAY
Moon Age Day 27   Moon Sign Aries

Your ability to influence financial matters in a positive way is sluggish under the current planetary influences. Still, you can tell yourself that the most important things in life have no monetary value. This is the Piscean spiritual ideal, but it might not prevent you from wanting those new shoes!

3 FRIDAY
Moon Age Day 28   Moon Sign Aries

Pisces is now in a very co-operative frame of mind. If you are not working today, you could definitely benefit from some time spent with groups of people who share your ideas and objectives. Later in the day you will find yourself in a very sociable frame of mind and won't want to spend Friday evening indoors.

4 SATURDAY
Moon Age Day 0   Moon Sign Taurus

As far as work and finances are concerned, the high-energy period continues today. You are extremely positive in your approach, a fact that rubs off on those around you. Co-operative ventures are especially well-starred now and your ability to work alongside others has rarely been better.

5 SUNDAY
Moon Age Day 1   Moon Sign Taurus

Turning your attention towards home once more, you discover someone doing all they can to make you feel particularly comfortable. Although this tends to take the wind out of your sails somewhat, you should be pleased by the attention you are receiving and on account of the genuine affection coming your way.

6 MONDAY
Moon Age Day 2   Moon Sign Taurus

Others will find you to be very talkative today and perhaps find it difficult to keep up with your active mind and quick tongue. You seem to be experiencing many extremes right now but you cope with them well. Certain family members could prove to be a little argumentative but this will not worry you unduly.

7 TUESDAY
Moon Age Day 3   Moon Sign Gemini

What a good day this would be for entertaining at home. It is clear that you are now at your vibrant best when in your own environment and will welcome others with open arms. Perhaps you will dream up an impromptu party or a gathering of some other sort. Avoid thinking too much about events beyond your own door now.

8 WEDNESDAY
Moon Age Day 4   Moon Sign Gemini

There are only so many things you can control at once, so if you are tiring with the strain of it all, delegate some of the responsibility. It looks as though there will be people around who are only too willing to lend a hand. Meanwhile, you can find new ways to fill your leisure hours.

9 THURSDAY
Moon Age Day 5   Moon Sign Cancer

You should be looking and feeling at your best today. Socially and romantically, there are many situations that seem tailor-made to suit your needs. Confrontations of any sort are now kept to a minimum and romance is number-one on the agenda of many sons and daughters of Pisces.

10 FRIDAY   *Moon Age Day 6   Moon Sign Cancer*

You can get the very best from family members and people you care for generally, even though it isn't possible for you to be at home quite as much as you might wish. A lot of the pressure you feel at the moment is related to being in the limelight, a place where you invariably feel ill at ease.

11 SATURDAY   *Moon Age Day 7   Moon Sign Leo*

Some quick thinking will come in handy today and you won't have any difficulty functioning at full strength. Your mind works quickly, though it is also sometimes drawn to places you care for deeply and which you might not have seen for a while. You should be feeling generally comfortable with personal and romantic relationships.

12 SUNDAY   *Moon Age Day 8   Moon Sign Leo*

Your mood and general peace of mind is assisted as a result of the actions of loved ones. This is a recurring theme at present and with so many good planetary positions it's not surprising. You may not feel the need to be doing something all the time and should be very happy to just relax today.

13 MONDAY   *Moon Age Day 9   Moon Sign Virgo*

Important decisions are best left alone for the moment, whilst you get on with negotiating the lunar low. Although you shouldn't really notice the Moon in Virgo quite so much this month, it can bring you to a more thoughtful stage in your life, a fact that your friends are apt to notice.

14 TUESDAY   *Moon Age Day 10   Moon Sign Virgo*

Unexpected delays are possible, allied to awkward people who seem to feel it is their duty to cause you certain headaches. You can deal with all of this and still come out smiling. The fact is that you have the bit between your teeth and it will take more than an adverse position of the Moon to hold you back.

15 WEDNESDAY   *Moon Age Day 11   Moon Sign Libra*

There is strength in numbers as far as you are concerned at the moment and you will be pleased to be in situations that allow you to co-operate with others. Although this isn't exactly the best of times in a financial sense, you can still find ways to make a few more pounds than you might have expected.

16 THURSDAY   *Moon Age Day 12   Moon Sign Libra*

Whilst nostalgic matters take on an agreeable aspect at this stage of the month, your home life should also seem to be rather exciting. Career issues could be less fortunate, especially if you are not using the necessary time and effort to keep things fully on course.

17 FRIDAY   *Moon Age Day 13   Moon Sign Scorpio*

You should now be able to express yourself very clearly and you won't have the least difficulty in getting your message across in the way you intend. The Sun is still in your solar third house, which has to be good for co-operative ventures of any sort and though you are happy in a group, you tend to lead it much of the time.

18 SATURDAY   *Moon Age Day 14   Moon Sign Scorpio*

Today you will probably not be completely in charge of practical matters and may have to defer to the opinions of people who seem to know better. All the same, don't take anything for granted because things are not always as they seem. Listening to your instincts helps you to make the right choices.

19 SUNDAY   *Moon Age Day 15   Moon Sign Scorpio*

Your mental skills are likely to increase around this time and it won't be at all difficult to work out how anyone is likely to react under given circumstances. Work according to your own mind and don't spend too much time thinking about what others would do. You are more than capable right now.

20 MONDAY   *Moon Age Day 16   Moon Sign Sagittarius*

Intellectual matters may now prove to be most rewarding and you will be chasing new ideas for most of today. The things that are going on out there in the wider world should be of particular interest and there isn't much doubt about your ability to adapt successfully to differing circumstances.

21 TUESDAY   *Moon Age Day 17   Moon Sign Sagittarius*

Influences could come along today that are almost certain to point you in the right direction when it comes to career and professional developments. That doesn't mean you are doing anything about them right now, however, because in the main you are likely to be more committed to social aspects on this particular day.

22 WEDNESDAY   *Moon Age Day 18   Moon Sign Capricorn*

Though you probably should avoid impulse purchases for the moment, there are bargains to be had if you look around carefully. You could also be on the receiving end of unexpected gifts from friends or loved ones. Financial deals can be turned in your favour with just a little extra thought on your part.

23 THURSDAY   *Moon Age Day 19   Moon Sign Capricorn*

Don't believe everything you hear today because not everyone will prove to be equally reliable. There are misleading influences around and it is possible you could spend quite some time walking down a path that leads to nothing but a dead end. Once again you need to call your intuition into play.

24 FRIDAY   *Moon Age Day 20   Moon Sign Aquarius*

Get tedious tasks out of the way early in the day, leaving yourself with the time to do what you want later. You should already be planning for what could be an excellent weekend but you will need to let others know your ideas early. By the evening you should be contemplating ways to please those you care for.

25 SATURDAY　　*Moon Age Day 21　　Moon Sign Aquarius*

Domestic matters should prove highly satisfying today, even if you are not making quite the practical progress you had hoped for. Romance is also on the cards and you are able to make a good impression on someone coming new into your life. Established relationships are likely to receive some sort of boost.

26 SUNDAY　　*Moon Age Day 22　　Moon Sign Aquarius*

There are new initiatives about. You can see them and know exactly how you ought to react but until the lunar high comes along tomorrow you would be better off planning than actually doing anything concrete. Other trends indicate that people you don't see often may make a return visit to your life.

27 MONDAY　　*Moon Age Day 23　　Moon Sign Pisces*

The Moon enters your zodiac sign, bringing one of the most productive and generally lucky periods of the month. Whatever you take on today, go for gold. Don't be shy of letting people know you are around and show even those people who think they know you well that there is more to you than meets the eye.

28 TUESDAY　　*Moon Age Day 24　　Moon Sign Pisces*

There is little time to rest today but that won't worry you much at all. You are at your best when out and about and certainly will not take kindly to being cooped up in the same place all day. Good luck is on your side and might bring a few surprises by the latter part of the day.

29 WEDNESDAY　　*Moon Age Day 25　　Moon Sign Aries*

A positive element is evident today, no matter what you decide to do. It could be that people who have proved to be somewhat awkward in the recent past are now taking a more considered attitude. On the other hand, it is possible that your persuasive powers are proving extremely useful with family members.

30 THURSDAY

Moon Age Day 26   Moon Sign Aries

In a domestic sense it appears that situations are looking good, though if life lacks a certain degree of sparkle you will need to move your mind and body out of the house. Excitement is possible but you are going to have to work a little to find it. Enlist the support of friends who think in a similar way to you.

31 FRIDAY

Moon Age Day 27   Moon Sign Aries

A far more personally enlivening period is now on the way. You should set out to show the world just who you are. Meanwhile, your personal creativity is likely to be going off the scale. Romance and leisure activities receive a definite boost at a time that ought to suit you in many different ways.

2019

1 SATURDAY
Moon Age Day 28   Moon Sign Taurus

Your power to get things done seems a little ineffectual today, so you may as well decide right at the start to take a little break. This is a time for thinking, with the acting part following in a couple of days. Don't be too worried if one or two of your plans seem to be going slightly wrong for now.

2 SUNDAY
Moon Age Day 29   Moon Sign Taurus

With a slight lull in the pace of activities, your mind could turn to house and home. What a good time this would be for entertaining and maybe for throwing a dinner party. Much of the enjoyment you experience today is likely to be associated with domestic rather than professional matters.

3 MONDAY
Moon Age Day 0   Moon Sign Gemini

Communication issues come to the fore today and you get by extremely well if you keep speaking. You may not always know exactly what you are talking about but in a way that doesn't matter. You are in the middle of a phase during which you could charm the birds down from the trees but not if you fail to communicate.

4 TUESDAY
Moon Age Day 1   Moon Sign Gemini

Stand by for a few potential irritations today, particularly where work is concerned. Maybe this comes of frustration because you can't get others to see your point of view. Remember that there is always more than one way of looking at any situation and show some of that stoical Piscean patience.

5 WEDNESDAY   *Moon Age Day 2   Moon Sign Cancer*

The focus now is definitely on your love life and romance generally. This is likely to be a very definite up period with much of what you have been looking for likely to come your way. Don't spoil this by spending more time than you have to out there in a more practical and go-getting world.

6 THURSDAY   *Moon Age Day 3   Moon Sign Cancer*

In terms of your general ego, today should turn out to be very interesting. This is one of the best days of the month for proving how much your own character can influence that of other people. Discussions at home go well and probably offer much more in a personal sense than outside influences.

7 FRIDAY   *Moon Age Day 4   Moon Sign Leo*

You could well be the main attraction wherever you go today. Make the most of it because for the next couple of days quieter times are in store. There are possible gains to be made financially, though this isn't the best time for gambling, unless you can be certain of the outcome – which you never can!

8 SATURDAY   *Moon Age Day 5   Moon Sign Leo*

Personal relationships could be somewhat less harmonious than you would wish now, although the fact doesn't seem to have a great deal to do with you. It's important to speak the truth at the moment, even if that means upsetting someone else. All the same, you can find ways to be tactful.

9 SUNDAY   *Moon Age Day 6   Moon Sign Virgo*

Keep your life today as free from complications as you can manage. There are some demands coming your way but as long as you are not expecting too much of yourself, you should be able to work through them. Some Pisceans are withdrawing into their shells at present so don't expect to be wonderful company.

10 MONDAY *Moon Age Day 7   Moon Sign Virgo*

It could feel as if you are taking one step forward but two steps back today. By tomorrow, any little cloud that seems to be hovering over your head will have lifted so there is no need to be out of sorts. Keep it simple and you won't even notice the lunar low.

11 TUESDAY *Moon Age Day 8   Moon Sign Virgo*

Since professional matters appear to be progressive enough, the chances are that you will want to put some pep into your out of work activities. Concern for the underdog is big in your thinking right now and you will be showing your usual Piscean support for charities that help people in need.

12 WEDNESDAY *Moon Age Day 9   Moon Sign Libra*

Some of your plans are now reaching a critical phase and you won't want to relinquish control to anyone else. This influence can directly interact with another – the need to share. Out of these conflicting interests you manage to forge a way forward that pleases you and everyone.

13 THURSDAY *Moon Age Day 10   Moon Sign Libra*

Prepare for a time of high spirits and joviality. Pisces has many positive aspects surrounding it right now and you can make the most of them. As much as anything, it is the way your mind is working that offers new ideas and ways to pass on the happiness you feel to those around you.

14 FRIDAY *Moon Age Day 11   Moon Sign Scorpio*

Much of your energy today is piled into situations you see as being personally important. It is just possible that this means less attention being put in the direction of family members. It would be good to offer a little reassurance because those you love are very used to seeing your warm and attentive side.

15 SATURDAY   *Moon Age Day 12   Moon Sign Scorpio*

You may now be feeling more boisterous than might have been the case of late. You stand out in a crowd and can give a very good impression of yourself. It is obvious that you are also quite adventurous at present, not a word that is often seen by the side of Pisces, so enjoy the change.

16 SUNDAY   *Moon Age Day 13   Moon Sign Sagittarius*

The current state of relationships in your life is likely to put a definite smile on your face. The Sun remains in your solar fourth house, which is good for all family matters and you should find that you can reach a consensus with people who have been quite awkward of late. Launch some new ideas at this time.

17 MONDAY   *Moon Age Day 14   Moon Sign Sagittarius*

Avoid minor conflicts with co-workers. These are not only unnecessary but get in the way of the sort of progress you should be making. Not everyone is on the same wavelength as you at the moment, no matter how hard you try to make it so. Some small financial gains could be in the offing later in the day.

18 TUESDAY   *Moon Age Day 15   Moon Sign Capricorn*

Your home life could bring a tendency towards laziness and for once you are happy to let others take some of the strain. It is important all the same to keep track of everything that's happening around you because there is a good chance of making some last minute decisions that will benefit you significantly.

19 WEDNESDAY   *Moon Age Day 16   Moon Sign Capricorn*

Today you will be ready to enjoy the lighter side of life and won't be taking anything all that seriously. Confident and talkative, you are a natural joker at the moment and can bring significant pleasure into the lives of others as you go about your business.

20 THURSDAY   *Moon Age Day 17   Moon Sign Capricorn*

There might be a slightly edgy atmosphere at work, something you will be doing your best to fight against throughout most of today. It is not likely to be you causing the problems, so rest assured that they probably won't have much of a bearing on your life if you choose to spend at least some time on your own.

21 FRIDAY   *Moon Age Day 18   Moon Sign Aquarius*

You may now find yourself involved in deeper emotional matters and you will also be making the most of domestic concerns and nostalgic situations. The Moon is in your solar twelfth house so there is likely to be quite a wistful side to your nature, though this situation changes quickly by Sunday.

22 SATURDAY   *Moon Age Day 19   Moon Sign Aquarius*

In a domestic sense life should be filled with contentment, though the Sun will soon change its position in your chart so you need to make the most of the homely trends. Professionally speaking, life will seem less interesting, which is why you need to use this time to please yourself in other ways.

23 SUNDAY   *Moon Age Day 20   Moon Sign Pisces*

With strong supporting planetary trends and the Moon paying your zodiac sign a visit, now is the moment to act. Objectives that have been in your sights for some time move forward at a pace, whilst at the same time you show yourself and everyone around you how dynamic and decisive you can be.

24 MONDAY   *Moon Age Day 21   Moon Sign Pisces*

The green light is still on and you find this a good time to make tracks, as well as gaining invaluable assistance on the way. General good luck attends your actions and offers you the chance to achieve something that has been at the back of your mind for a while. Even if life isn't easy, it should be very interesting.

25 TUESDAY *Moon Age Day 22   Moon Sign Pisces*

You have what it takes to move mountains, though only at your own speed. Don't be rushed at present and be willing to take your time in getting where you want to be. Pisces needs extra stimulus now, particularly in a romantic sense and you may also be ringing the changes with regard to friendship.

26 WEDNESDAY *Moon Age Day 23   Moon Sign Aries*

Attention is now focused on your own ego, which is probably stronger than it has been for quite some time. You will take great delight in entertaining others and won't be in the least concerned if the spotlight is upon you. Pisces needs to shine sometimes and it looks as though this is such a period.

27 THURSDAY *Moon Age Day 24   Moon Sign Aries*

Whatever is happening in your relationship at present should prove to be both happy and exciting. Romantic encounters could come thick and fast for those Pisceans who have been looking for love, while if you are in a committed partnership, you will find ways to pep it up and to bring in some excitement.

28 FRIDAY *Moon Age Day 25   Moon Sign Taurus*

You might have to struggle somewhat today to keep work matters on track and would do well to accept the proffered advice and help of colleagues. If you insist on going it alone, you will work twice as hard and probably still not achieve your objectives. Too much pride is definitely not a good thing at the moment.

29 SATURDAY *Moon Age Day 26   Moon Sign Taurus*

Places of entertainment are a must at the start of this weekend. It isn't out of the question that you have chosen this time to take a break, in which case you can travel wherever takes your fancy. Even if you are stuck with the usual routines you can find ways to alter them and to make life more interesting.

30 SUNDAY

Moon Age Day 27   Moon Sign Gemini

Your love life is positively highlighted on this last Sunday in June. Spend some time with the person who means the most to you and you won't regret it. Seek out intelligent conversation and avoid noisy or irksome people. You might decide the time is right to take a short journey to somewhere particularly interesting.

July

2019

1 MONDAY
Moon Age Day 28   Moon Sign Gemini

Love and romance are likely to be uppermost in your mind at present and they continue to be so for a few days to come. It pays to extend your social life too by going out and meeting new people. Freedom is important whilst the Sun occupies your solar fifth house, where it will be for the next two weeks and more.

2 TUESDAY
Moon Age Day 0   Moon Sign Gemini

Life brings excitement for many Pisceans now. There are likely to be sudden changes of direction and a desire to do things simply for the thrill. Your spirit is unfettered at the moment and when Pisces is in this frame of mind, anything at all is possible. Friends should be especially co-operative.

3 WEDNESDAY
Moon Age Day 1   Moon Sign Cancer

Romance can seem larger than life itself. Pisceans may well be in an overly nostalgic mood for today and that can bring its own little problems. Make sure you retain a degree of realism, even though the present position of the Moon makes that rather difficult. In a practical sense new options could open up at work.

4 THURSDAY
Moon Age Day 2   Moon Sign Cancer

Today could turn out to be quite an exceptional period and one during which it is very important that you get away from your usual routines in order to meet new people. The greater the stimulus that comes into your life at the moment the better you will respond. Ordinary situations will seem quite boring.

114

5 FRIDAY
Moon Age Day 3   Moon Sign Leo

You can most likely trust your intuition right now, which may be giving you a good insight into the personal dilemmas your friends are going through. Handing out advice is easy for Pisces at the best of times but especially so under present trends. Save time later in the day to do something for yourself.

6 SATURDAY
Moon Age Day 4   Moon Sign Leo

Back your hunches when it comes to financial transactions and don't be put off by setbacks. There could be some good luck around later in the day so it might be a mistake to try to sort out too much early on. You don't lack the confidence to do the right thing, though one or two people could prove awkward at the moment.

7 SUNDAY
Moon Age Day 5   Moon Sign Virgo

You might be frustrated by the lack of assistance that comes from the direction of other people. As your patience runs low you will need to try to keep life as simple as possible. Routines will appear tedious and yet you don't have the ability to break out of them. Try to stay calm if you can and ride out the trend.

8 MONDAY
☿   *Moon Age Day 6   Moon Sign Virgo*

Your energy is still lacking, but if that worries you, bear in mind that the lunar low only lasts for a couple of days. Don't focus on everything you're not doing, but instead think in terms of forward planning. Knocking your head against a brick wall isn't likely to help at all under present trends.

9 TUESDAY
☿   *Moon Age Day 7   Moon Sign Libra*

The potential for a new romantic interest is formidable. This is a period during which you have stunning powers of attraction and a magnetism that others find difficult to avoid. The only slightly negative side of this is that you might be attracting the wrong sort of attention – which could lead to a little embarrassment all round.

10 WEDNESDAY ☿   *Moon Age Day 8*   *Moon Sign Libra*

Get an early start on work projects. Your excess of energy should ensure that much can be accomplished, especially as no one should get in your way. Keep an your eye on your ultimate objectives. Life can be like an emotional seesaw at present and it is sometimes difficult to get the breaks.

11 THURSDAY ☿   *Moon Age Day 9*   *Moon Sign Scorpio*

You need to impose some order on your working life because so many details right now can seem nebulous and even impossible. Self-discipline seems to be the way forward. Concentrate on one thing at a time and don't be inclined to dissipate your energies by having to go back and put right mistakes all the time.

12 FRIDAY ☿   *Moon Age Day 10*   *Moon Sign Scorpio*

There is an expansive element at work and you should be able to co-operate fully with colleagues. Pisceans who are between jobs at the moment should concentrate a good deal of their energy into looking around because there are likely to be options on offer. This would not be the best day to gamble with finances.

13 SATURDAY ☿ *Moon Age Day 11*   *Moon Sign Sagittarius*

You shouldn't take anything for granted now on a personal level. You won't be everyone's cup of tea today but you need to be realistic and to avoid reactions that are out of proportion with reality. Spending a little time on your own might feel attractive today, but you would be better off finding some enjoyment with friends.

14 SUNDAY ☿ *Moon Age Day 12*   *Moon Sign Sagittarius*

Now you can improve your lot by being in touch with people who inspire you. There are many possibilities that present themselves right now and in terms of your professional life you are showing a greater amount of initiative. Hunches are worth a punt because you have the ability to follow them through.

15 MONDAY ☿ *Moon Age Day 13   Moon Sign Capricorn*

Recent efforts now begin to show positive results. You gain more control over your working environment and you should discover assistance coming from directions you never realised. You can enlist valuable support from a number of different people and should be quite keen to put in that extra effort that will make all the difference.

16 TUESDAY ☿ *Moon Age Day 14   Moon Sign Capricorn*

You still need to get ahead with plans, though you are inclined to realise that this might sometimes take a very considered and careful approach. Today Pisces is likely to be looking around, waiting for the best opportunity to act and then doing all that is necessary to win through.

17 WEDNESDAY ☿ *Moon Age Day 15   Moon Sign Capricorn*

Certain personal or practical arrangements could quite easily be subject to delay now. If this is the case, be flexible and willing to take a different path at very short notice. Casual conversations can bring unexpected news or some really good ideas you will soon be bursting to put into practice.

18 THURSDAY ☿ *Moon Age Day 16   Moon Sign Aquarius*

Stay around familiar faces today because you are not feeling adventurous now. Although you are by no means a shrinking violet, you could be rather inclined to hide behind the bigger personalities of friends. But it doesn't matter what you do, there are people who want to know you better.

19 FRIDAY ☿ *Moon Age Day 17   Moon Sign Aquarius*

It shouldn't be too difficult to impress others today and you manage to pull the right rabbit out of the hat when it is important to do so. People will trust you a great deal, leading you to worry just a little in case you let them down. This is most unlikely to happen. Just be yourself and do what feels right.

20 SATURDAY   ☿   *Moon Age Day 18*   *Moon Sign Pisces*

Along comes the lunar high, and together with existing planetary trends it is likely to increase your persuasive powers no end. Personal partnerships should improve too and it seems as though you have the magic formula when it comes to getting on with just about anyone you come across today.

21 SUNDAY   ☿   *Moon Age Day 19*   *Moon Sign Pisces*

Stand by for a phase during which you will be showing a great deal of charisma and personal attractiveness. There could be new opportunities for romance and the lunar high continues to support you in your efforts to get ahead. With everything to play for, this is the time to let your light shine.

22 MONDAY   ☿   *Moon Age Day 20*   *Moon Sign Pisces*

When it matters the most you can rely on your instincts today, which are most unlikely to let you down. A few financial pressures are possible this week but there are many things you can do that are absolutely free, or which cost very little. Being with friends would be good but even better times involve your partner.

23 TUESDAY   ☿   *Moon Age Day 21*   *Moon Sign Aries*

Around the time the Sun enters your solar sixth house, you can expect to experience a boost to your health and feelings of general wellbeing. If you have been off colour, this position of the Sun is quite likely to help. Practical projects and plans for the future are also aided by the presence of the Sun here.

24 WEDNESDAY   ☿   *Moon Age Day 22*   *Moon Sign Aries*

Progress is likely to be swift now, mainly because you work hard to get things done. It doesn't matter whether there is a professional aspect to today or not, simply because your capacity for work demonstrates itself as much at home as it does anywhere else. Don't forget that you also need to have some fun.

25 THURSDAY ☿ *Moon Age Day 23 Moon Sign Taurus*

Get out and travel as much as you can today. You won't take kindly to being stuck indoors and you can gain tremendously from seeing new places, as well as from meeting people you haven't come across before. If at all possible, avoid taking on an excessive or stressful workload.

26 FRIDAY ☿ *Moon Age Day 24 Moon Sign Taurus*

Seek out the new and unusual in life and concentrate on using the natural detective qualities within your deep Piscean personality. Anything that captivates your interest at present is grist to the mill, the most important fact being that you see clearly through any form of subterfuge.

27 SATURDAY ☿ *Moon Age Day 25 Moon Sign Taurus*

Although you are still a strong participant in the game of life, you also have the power to stand back from situations and to look at them dispassionately. The weekend brings its own brand of fun, even if your sense of humour at present is slightly off the wall and distinctly unusual when seen from the perspective of others.

28 SUNDAY ☿ *Moon Age Day 26 Moon Sign Gemini*

You are in a light and optimistic mood, anxious to get to know new people but also very attentive to family members and friends. With such a sociable period in operation, it might be rather difficult to actually get anything done in a concrete sense. Never mind, you can easily split your time.

29 MONDAY ☿ *Moon Age Day 27 Moon Sign Gemini*

Having friends close to you now is very important and makes you feel better about yourself. Although there could be one or two slightly sticky situations to get through today, you keep a smile on your face and show how positive you are. Your confidence might be lacking but nobody would ever guess.

30 TUESDAY ☿ *Moon Age Day 28* *Moon Sign Cancer*

This would be a great day for family gatherings and for talking over old times. Although you are still progressive and productive, you are more likely to show your sociable side. Some advantages may be gained by sharing some of your innermost thoughts with those you know to be trustworthy.

31 WEDNESDAY ☿ *Moon Age Day 0* *Moon Sign Cancer*

It isn't that you are following good trends today, more that you are able to create them as you go along. This is especially true in a career sense or with regard to an important personal interest if you are not working at present. Most important of all at the moment is your cheerfulness and sunny disposition.

2019

1 THURSDAY
Moon Age Day 1   Moon Sign Leo

You should be well supported in matters undertaken as part of a team, and friends may help to put your personal life into a better context. This is definitely a day on which you should co-operate and during which you can get a great deal done. You may be glad to find you are nearing the end of a specific task that has weighed on your mind.

2 FRIDAY
Moon Age Day 2   Moon Sign Leo

Trends place a strong focus on luxury and the good things in life coming along for this Friday. Get out with friends or relatives because you perform better in groups as far as social trends are concerned. You tend to act very much on impulse right now but that's no bad thing in the short-term.

3 SATURDAY
Moon Age Day 3   Moon Sign Virgo

A desire to escape responsibility could be the temporary response to the lunar low. As the effect of the Moon comes into play, you are now more willing than ever to let those around you take the lead. Some people may find this difficult to understand, but your kind nature should win out in the end.

4 SUNDAY
Moon Age Day 4   Moon Sign Virgo

Your capabilities may not be up to the mark today, or at least that is the way you are likely to feel. Don't take on more than is reasonable and give yourself the time you need to rest. There are people in your immediate vicinity who have some important, and possibly even slightly shocking, revelations to impart.

5 MONDAY
Moon Age Day 5   Moon Sign Libra

You have strong support when you make choices today, especially at work. Colleagues should be doing all they can to fall in line with your opinions and it is clear that your mind is focused. When you are not at work, intellectual pursuits of one sort or another are most likely to appeal to you.

6 TUESDAY
Moon Age Day 6   Moon Sign Libra

Though intimate relationships now seem settled and cheerful, there could be one or two small problems with family members or friends. The problem is that you find it temporarily difficult to get on-side with those who seem determined to throw a spanner in the works. Your usual patience is the key.

7 WEDNESDAY
Moon Age Day 7   Moon Sign Scorpio

If you take the initiative in matters of the heart, you may get a payback in the form of achieving a longed-for objective that might have looked a long way off. Don't get tied down with petty rules and regulations at this time. You need a clear horizon during which you can do more or less whatever pleases you.

8 THURSDAY
Moon Age Day 8   Moon Sign Scorpio

By focusing on the detail, you should be able to get all manner of things sorted out today. Your ability to see into the very heart of matters gives you extra influence, as well as the power to change them if necessary. You now rely less on the opinions of others, no matter how well intentioned they are.

9 FRIDAY
Moon Age Day 9   Moon Sign Sagittarius

If a new relationship puts you under pressure try not to react too strongly, especially if you feel you are being goaded. It should be easy to get your own way if you employ a few psychological tactics. There are some unusual trends around at the moment and that means a rather different sort of day.

10 SATURDAY   *Moon Age Day 10   Moon Sign Sagittarius*

Your social prospects appear to be far more rewarding than might have been the case for the last few days. Don't be too keen to take on new challenges, at least until tomorrow. Someone you see very rarely could be making an appearance in your life and they offer bright and enticing incentives.

11 SUNDAY   *Moon Age Day 11   Moon Sign Sagittarius*

Work and practical matters will probably occupy your mind a good deal today. There is a strong atmosphere of co-operation around you and you enjoy yourself when you are with people whose minds work along the same track as yours. You have the confidence to push yourself forward, either now or at the start of a new week.

12 MONDAY   *Moon Age Day 12   Moon Sign Capricorn*

The greater your social interests today, the more you will enjoy everything that is on offer. Joint ventures should go well, whether these are associated with work or leisure. You still have the confidence to say and do the right thing, and you will probably find that you are meeting a stream of interesting and stimulating people.

13 TUESDAY   *Moon Age Day 13   Moon Sign Capricorn*

A continued planetary high influencing social interest is forecast for today. You won't want to get bogged down with tasks you hate and will need to leave certain matters until another day. Even if you are nearing the end of a phase in your life there is no need to rush to complete it. Take your time.

14 WEDNESDAY   *Moon Age Day 14   Moon Sign Aquarius*

You can expect the unexpected as far as your love life is concerned now. You may not feel that you are getting your own way but in the end you should be able to bring people round to your point of view. Entertaining might be fun and you will be doing your best to enjoy what the summer has to offer.

15 THURSDAY   *Moon Age Day 15   Moon Sign Aquarius*

This is a time of physical efficiency during which you are burning up masses of energy and doing yourself some good on the way. Others will find it difficult to maintain the same sort of pace you are setting and will be surprised by your attitudes and actions around now.

16 FRIDAY   *Moon Age Day 16   Moon Sign Aquarius*

Look very carefully for opportunities for advancement – they are there if you look hard enough. Life isn't especially easy today but you are competent, discriminating and able to get what you want with perseverance. The more romantic aspects of your life are likely to be quite gratifying.

17 SATURDAY   *Moon Age Day 17   Moon Sign Pisces*

If you pull a few strings at work or at home you should be able to progress quickly and to get what you want from life in most ways. The lunar high gives you the ability to chance your arm with every likelihood of success. People will listen to what you are saying and automatically trust your judgement.

18 SUNDAY   *Moon Age Day 18   Moon Sign Pisces*

There is an enhancement to relationships brought about by the present position of the Moon. This is the time to tell others exactly how you feel about them and a period during which you will be firing on all cylinders. Don't wait to be asked because you have to take the initiative as much as possible now.

19 MONDAY   *Moon Age Day 19   Moon Sign Aries*

This is still a good period to be making the sort of progress you are definitely looking for at this time. You show good and promising judgement and won't easily be put off, once you have made up your mind to follow a particular path. Inspiration is part of the present package.

20 TUESDAY
Moon Age Day 20   Moon Sign Aries

Don't get involved in needless debates, which won't help your cause and can only serve to confuse already problematic situations. There is help on offer if you want it, though you are likely to be relying on your own efforts and judgement now and so may decide to continue going it alone.

21 WEDNESDAY
Moon Age Day 21   Moon Sign Aries

The smooth running of practical affairs today is your chief concern, as indeed seems to have been the case for a while now. Although circumstances force you to work within certain confines, you are presently extremely good at solving problems and won't easily be distracted, even by people you have little time for.

22 THURSDAY
Moon Age Day 22   Moon Sign Taurus

Help seems available to you today no matter what you decide to do. There are times when you are responding to necessity rather than to choice, but you can make this enjoyable too. Routines could be a bore, which is why you are doing your best to ring the changes as much as you can.

23 FRIDAY
Moon Age Day 23   Moon Sign Taurus

In personal relationships, it is important not to get too wrapped up in your own ideas, no matter how entrancing they seem to you. Use your listening ear and be willing to modify your plans if necessary. A final word of warning for a summer Friday – avoid staying in the same place for too long at a time.

24 SATURDAY
Moon Age Day 24   Moon Sign Gemini

Home is the best and most comfortable place for Pisces to be at present, so this weekend probably won't see you moving around all that much. You are quite creative at the moment so will most likely be working in your house or garden. A degree of personal contentment is present at this time.

25 SUNDAY   *Moon Age Day 25   Moon Sign Gemini*

You are clearly open to new input this Sunday and would be pleased to try things you have shied away from in the past. There are some interesting characters around and you are not the least amongst them. With a great urge to seek fresh fields and pastures new, this is the best time of all to think about a holiday.

26 MONDAY   *Moon Age Day 26   Moon Sign Cancer*

You should detect noticeable improvements in one-to-one relationships, and this can apply even if you had thought everything was fine anyway. Rules and regulations won't impress you much at the start of this working week but you will be able to tell others what they should be doing with no difficulty.

27 TUESDAY   *Moon Age Day 27   Moon Sign Cancer*

Make the most of the fact that your powers of attraction are in the ascendant. If you are single, you should find attention coming from a number of different directions, though of course this could be the case even if you are not single. Responsibilities are for the birds right now.

28 WEDNESDAY   *Moon Age Day 28   Moon Sign Leo*

Your best area of influence today is in one-to-one relationships and these don't necessarily have to be of the romantic sort. Self-employed Pisceans are particularly in luck now, with the chance to stretch yourself and maybe some financial help coming along, either now or in the near future.

29 THURSDAY   *Moon Age Day 29   Moon Sign Leo*

Whatever you decide to do today, embark on it as if it were some grand adventure. You are in the part of the year that is especially good for travel and you will especially enjoy today if you are not at work. With a really good attitude to life, it seems as though the world is your oyster wherever you happen to be.

30 FRIDAY   *Moon Age Day 0   Moon Sign Virgo*

With a little financial good fortune likely to come your way around now it is possible you will be able to spoil yourself. That's fine because Pisces is up for a little luxury. You are especially creative at the moment and so may decide the time is right for some fairly major changes at home.

31 SATURDAY   *Moon Age Day 1   Moon Sign Virgo*

Although there are obstacles to overcome today, you deal with them easily and leave yourself feeling quite satisfied with your general progress. Your imaginative faculties are especially good right now, which makes it easy for you to look and plan ahead. Friends should prove to be very supportive.

1 SUNDAY
Moon Age Day 2   Moon Sign Libra

You might be up against a few challenges when it comes to keeping yourself organised today. It's late in the year for a spring clean but that is what elements of your life actually need. Don't burden yourself with too many obligations because you need the time to straighten out whatever is bothering you.

2 MONDAY
Moon Age Day 3   Moon Sign Libra

Some of your most successful hours of the month are likely to come along today as you work alongside others. You may now benefit from the co-operation that might have been missing in working relationships recently. Away from the professional scene, you are happy to accommodate the wishes of family members.

3 TUESDAY
Moon Age Day 4   Moon Sign Scorpio

Try to avoid pointless conflicts in relationships or at work. You are not really in the mood to throw yourself fully into any situation that means aggression or confusion. There are ways around any situation if you look carefully and today offers plenty in the way of personal happiness, even if practical situations are difficult.

4 WEDNESDAY
Moon Age Day 5   Moon Sign Scorpio

You can enjoy an improved social and romantic period whilst the Sun remains in your solar seventh house. The odd, the unusual and the downright weird have a particular fascination for you under present trends, so don't be surprised if at least a few people look at you askance around this time.

5 THURSDAY   *Moon Age Day 6   Moon Sign Scorpio*

There seems to be plenty of potential for good times in all relationships now. It should be easy to make new friends and you should be the flavour of the month as far as most people are concerned. Your natural shyness won't be an obstacle under present trends and you practically shine in social situations.

6 FRIDAY   *Moon Age Day 7   Moon Sign Sagittarius*

You might try to bring a bit more subtlety to certain situations today, though lacking this particular skill is not generally a problem for your birth sign. There is just a possibility that you are not fully taking into account the strength of feeling coming from others. A little more attention might be in order.

7 SATURDAY   *Moon Age Day 8   Moon Sign Sagittarius*

Creative self-expression is an important factor in your life around this time. Exciting social and romantic opportunities exist for the weekend, though you will have to make the most of them and shouldn't hold back when it comes to seizing the moment. The fulfilment of a particular wish is high on your agenda.

8 SUNDAY   *Moon Age Day 9   Moon Sign Capricorn*

Exercise some caution when you are dealing with people you know to be a little touchy. It isn't anything you are doing that throws a spanner in the works but there may be difficulties associated with close relationships. It might be better to spend more time with friends today and less with relatives.

9 MONDAY   *Moon Age Day 10   Moon Sign Capricorn*

The time has come to put a great deal of effort into establishing your own security. Wherever any setbacks arise you need to remain positive because it is possible you are not showing enough confidence in yourself under present trends. Friends can be especially warm and loving – and in some cases stifling.

10 TUESDAY   *Moon Age Day 11   Moon Sign Aquarius*

You may well have good, practical ideas for professional advancement but putting them into action is likely to prove just a little problematic now. Be discriminating and even a little ruthless if you really want to get on well. Tell yourself that you deserve to be listened to because in the main it's true.

11 WEDNESDAY   *Moon Age Day 12   Moon Sign Aquarius*

There are good social trends influencing this midweek period. An excellent opportunity exists to form new friendships and to strengthen personal and romantic ties. What you won't want to do much today is finish off jobs in and around your home, especially ones that are without personal interest for you.

12 THURSDAY   *Moon Age Day 13   Moon Sign Aquarius*

Work-wise and financially, your power to attract just the right circumstances remains particularly strong. The same positive trends surround your personal life and it is likely that romance flourishes at the moment. Conventions might not seem so appealing and there is little doubt that you are now doing your own thing.

13 FRIDAY   *Moon Age Day 14   Moon Sign Pisces*

Things change rapidly this month and today is no exception. The lunar high transforms your mood so much it is like being fired from a cannon. All your enthusiasm comes together to allow forward progress in a number of different ways. Friends offer some very important practical assistance.

14 SATURDAY   *Moon Age Day 15   Moon Sign Pisces*

This would be an excellent time to take a leading role and to show people what you are made of. There's nothing quiet about Pisces today and you are willing to share your unique ideas with anyone who will listen. You can also afford to push your luck more than you have so far this month.

15 SUNDAY
Moon Age Day 16   Moon Sign Aries

This is a time for renewal and a period during which you can dump anything that hasn't been working the way you would have wished. If this seems a little cavalier and perhaps even brutal, just think about what will happen if you keep working on projects that don't have a hope of working out the way you would wish.

16 MONDAY
Moon Age Day 17   Moon Sign Aries

In practical matters, there is plenty to keep you busy and you can expect a fairly good day, even if not everyone is behaving in quite the way you might have expected. Keep a sense of proportion, especially when it comes to looking at matters that might involve financial decisions.

17 TUESDAY
Moon Age Day 18   Moon Sign Aries

A generally agreeable period lies ahead of you. If it isn't exciting enough, the chances are you have not done all you could to pep things up. Friends are not especially predictable at this stage and there will be some leading questions to ask if you really want to know what is going on.

18 WEDNESDAY
Moon Age Day 19   Moon Sign Taurus

If your partner proves less agreeable than usual, maybe you should look for the reason within yourself. Have you forgotten an anniversary or some other important event? Make a few kind gestures but don't go overboard, otherwise it might look as though you are crawling.

19 THURSDAY
Moon Age Day 20   Moon Sign Taurus

Only attempt today what you really know is likely to work and stay well clear of gambling or signing documents you don't really understand. If there are major purchases in the offing, try to leave them until tomorrow but if that proves to be impossible, check the details carefully and maybe take a friend along for support and advice.

20 FRIDAY *Moon Age Day 21   Moon Sign Gemini*

Remember there is only so much you can control on your own. The more you are willing to co-operate today, the better things are likely to go for you. It doesn't matter how hard you try, in the eyes of a very few people everything you do is wrong. Simply try to ignore negative people and stick with reasonable ones.

21 SATURDAY *Moon Age Day 22   Moon Sign Gemini*

In personal encounters, your competitive nature is stimulated. This is no problem as long as your opposite number knows how to lose gracefully. It seems as though there are very few demands you would shy away from on this Saturday but make sure you avoid taking on more than is reasonable.

22 SUNDAY *Moon Age Day 23   Moon Sign Gemini*

A fairly progressive phase continues and you have plenty of power at your fingertips on those occasions you need it the most. When it comes to forward planning, you are second to none. Give way to the ideas of your partner, or to someone you count as a really good and loyal friend.

23 MONDAY *Moon Age Day 24   Moon Sign Cancer*

Now the Sun moves into your solar eighth house. During the next month or so you can expect the end of certain phases in your life and the beginning of new ones. This position of the Sun might also bring out the detective in you, making you seek to know how everything works.

24 TUESDAY *Moon Age Day 25   Moon Sign Cancer*

If you know you are telling the truth today, it is important to say so. This is necessary even if you know you could upset someone else on the way. The problems will be much greater if you refuse to open your mouth now and will only mean some really harsh words further down the line.

25 WEDNESDAY
Moon Age Day 26   Moon Sign Leo

Some very enjoyable things may be taking place at work. It should be easy to get on the right side of superiors because charm is your middle name at present. Don't go too far, though, because your actions must be both believable and sincere.

26 THURSDAY
Moon Age Day 27   Moon Sign Leo

Instinct and intuition guide you through a period that requires you to react at a moment's notice. The magnetic side of your Piscean personality is now fully on display and it is clear that you are out to impress in some way. Any element of tedium in your life right now is likely to be shunned instantly.

27 FRIDAY
Moon Age Day 28   Moon Sign Virgo

There is likely to be a degree of uncertainty around for the next couple of days. This comes from the position of the Moon in your opposite zodiac sign. Instead of getting on with anything new, deal with situations that are nearly resolved and clear the decks for actions that come early next week.

28 SATURDAY
Moon Age Day 0   Moon Sign Virgo

Get as much rest as you can today and avoid being stressed by taking on more than is necessary. You could be a little short-tempered and certainly won't have the amount of patience that you usually have. Your imagination remains strong, a fact that can prove to be of tremendous use in all sorts of ways.

29 SUNDAY
Moon Age Day 1   Moon Sign Libra

You enjoy a fairly high profile at the moment, particularly in social situations. It looks as though you can shine like a star when the mood takes you but on the other hand, you will be fairly sulky if you are prevailed upon to do anything that really goes against the grain.

30 MONDAY
Moon Age Day 2   Moon Sign Libra

It is very important to be in the right place at the right time today, something you should instinctively know how to do. You should be fairly confident and not half as likely to make unforced errors as is sometimes the case. If you feel anxious about a task you have to do, enlist a little support.

October 2019

1 TUESDAY
Moon Age Day 3   Moon Sign Scorpio

Everyday progress may be upset as emotional issues come along to shake your equilibrium. How you react to these is entirely up to you but there isn't much point in allowing them to rule your day. If you must worry about anything, set yourself a time limit for doing so and then get on with other things.

2 WEDNESDAY
Moon Age Day 4   Moon Sign Scorpio

You should be feeling mentally strong today and in the right frame of mind to tackle a few issues that might have intimidated you in the past. Nothing is missed as you push forward on all fronts and show the world that you are capable of being a go-getter. You might need to be a little more circumspect in romantic matters.

3 THURSDAY
Moon Age Day 5   Moon Sign Sagittarius

This would be an excellent day for bringing almost any sort of matter to a head but you need to take care how you go about doing it. The fact is that you lack some of your usual tact and won't be half as understanding as people expect you to be. Try to show a little sympathy if someone makes a mistake.

4 FRIDAY
Moon Age Day 6   Moon Sign Sagittarius

Relationships could be subject to intense emotional pressure today. Keep a sense of proportion and try to be steady in your reactions. What you don't need at the moment is other people telling you how you should react under any given circumstance. All the same, you need to be careful not to fire off at them.

5 SATURDAY   *Moon Age Day 7   Moon Sign Capricorn*

You should now be able to build upon recent successes and the weekend, though sometimes making great demands on you, is one that you will find to be useful and in some way different. Don't get bogged down by details, especially in social matters. You can easily get to where you want to go, though you have to be flexible.

6 SUNDAY   *Moon Age Day 8   Moon Sign Capricorn*

Pressures that exist around you generally leave you unfazed. You have what it takes to rise above situations that normally pressure you and you tend to smile a great deal today. When Pisces is optimistic, almost anything becomes possible and you won't have any trouble attracting a good deal of positive attention.

7 MONDAY   *Moon Age Day 9   Moon Sign Capricorn*

Personal ambitions are slightly less focused than you might wish but that doesn't really matter at a time when you are taking a broad overview of life. Concentrate on what you know you can do well at work but by the time the evening comes along, you will probably want to try something new.

8 TUESDAY   *Moon Age Day 10   Moon Sign Aquarius*

A bout of sheer optimism seems to be overtaking you. This is a bit of a roller coaster of a month when it comes to your attitude to life and that makes it somewhat difficult for others to keep up with you. You might surprise one or two people with your determination to be cheerful today.

9 WEDNESDAY   *Moon Age Day 11   Moon Sign Aquarius*

Make up your mind now about proposed career changes and if you cannot do so, look to the advice of people who know the situation and also know you. In the end you have to choose for yourself but the different perspective that can be brought to bear by friends could still be very useful.

10 THURSDAY   *Moon Age Day 12   Moon Sign Pisces*

This should be a fairly lucky time and a period during which things tend to fall into place of their own accord. You can gain support from those who are higher up the ladder than you are and you find yourself in the middle of a get-up-and-go interlude that offers new incentives throughout the day.

11 FRIDAY   *Moon Age Day 13   Moon Sign Pisces*

The green light is on and there is no reason at all why you should not be getting on very well in most areas of your life. You have a natural tendency to take up an issue and run with it. Those around you recognise this and should be more than happy to follow your lead in most matters.

12 SATURDAY   *Moon Age Day 14   Moon Sign Pisces*

You should be entering a more mentally fulfilling interlude and the sense of movement in your life is likely to be very welcome. You won't hold fast to what you know but instead be willing to change when necessary. A definite breeze of opportunity seems to be blowing through your life.

13 SUNDAY   *Moon Age Day 15   Moon Sign Aries*

A friend might have some inspiring news. Even if this doesn't have a bearing on your life you will be pleased for them. There are excellent trends around that tell you to have a chat with someone you like. You don't actually have to achieve anything at all today because life seems to be arranging itself pretty effectively.

14 MONDAY   *Moon Age Day 16   Moon Sign Aries*

When it comes to discussions and debate a very relaxed atmosphere now prevails. There have been times so far during October when you were tense and didn't communicate quite as well as you might. Those times are now over and you commit yourself fully to co-operation and to seeing the other person's point of view.

15 TUESDAY   *Moon Age Day 17   Moon Sign Taurus*

There is every reason to believe that life will be going your way at the moment. Most circumstances seem to be working to your distinct advantage but a lot of this is down to your own positive attitude. Creative potential is especially good and you have what it takes to turn heads in a personal sense.

16 WEDNESDAY   *Moon Age Day 18   Moon Sign Taurus*

A personal matter is likely to put you on the defensive today but do make sure you are not defending yourself before you have even been attacked. The people who matter the most will be on your side at the moment and are unlikely to let you down, even if the going gets a little difficult.

17 THURSDAY   *Moon Age Day 19   Moon Sign Taurus*

This should be a potentially wonderful time in terms of personal relationships. There are quite a few planetary aspects and positions now working in your favour and very little to get in the way of romantic bliss. If you are not involved in a relationship right now, perhaps you should be keeping your eyes open.

18 FRIDAY   *Moon Age Day 20   Moon Sign Gemini*

If you have to rethink a particular plan of action, don't see this as being necessarily bad. On the contrary, the more you rush into things right now, the greater is the likelihood of making a mistake. People you haven't seen for quite some time could be making a renewed appearance in your life.

19 SATURDAY   *Moon Age Day 21   Moon Sign Gemini*

This may be the best time of this month to have a clear out in your life. It could be that there are certain business or social relationships that have been holding you back or people who simply don't seem to have your best interests at heart. You are far from being hard-hearted but may be forced by circumstance to look hard at situations.

20 SUNDAY — *Moon Age Day 22   Moon Sign Cancer*

Any outdoor pursuits you may follow are especially well highlighted now, as the more sporting and competitive side of your nature also beings to show itself. Because you are feeling somewhat brave at present you may choose to tackle an issue that has had you quaking in your boots at some stage in the past.

21 MONDAY — *Moon Age Day 23   Moon Sign Cancer*

An answer to any romantic yearnings is possible now and if you are a Pisces who is looking for a new relationship, this is one of those days when your wishes just could come true. In a more mundane sense you are now pretty much in charge of your own destiny so put in that extra bit of effort that counts.

22 TUESDAY — *Moon Age Day 24   Moon Sign Leo*

Whilst this is a good time to enjoy a sense of personal freedom, one or two of your more outrageous schemes may have to be reined in a little. Give yourself a pat on the back if you have recently unearthed a significant bargain but don't stop shopping because this phase hasn't ended yet.

23 WEDNESDAY — *Moon Age Day 25   Moon Sign Leo*

With a greater sense of freedom and adventure than you have experienced for some weeks, it looks as though this part of October is turning very much to your advantage. Your increased confidence and urge to get on well, both practically and socially, assist you to make the most of today's positive planetary trends.

24 THURSDAY — *Moon Age Day 26   Moon Sign Virgo*

Trends move on and today the lunar low bears down on you. All the same, your chart retains plenty of supporting planets, which could mean that apart from a slight tendency to look on the negative side, the Moon has very little bearing on your life at this time. Don't slow down where major efforts are concerned.

25 FRIDAY   *Moon Age Day 27   Moon Sign Virgo*

They say a change is as good as a rest and that certainly seems to be the case as far as you are concerned. There is no sense in trying to keep track of everything that is going on around you and it would be advantageous to allow others to take some of the strain in matters that are not of supreme importance.

26 SATURDAY   *Moon Age Day 28   Moon Sign Libra*

Your desire for personal freedom is very strong. This can make you something of a loose cannon on occasions because people who think they know you well are likely to be constantly surprised by your actions and reactions. It doesn't do any harm at all to keep the world guessing once in a while.

27 SUNDAY   *Moon Age Day 0   Moon Sign Libra*

This is a marvellous period to get out into the social world and make sure that your voice is heard. You can expect to make some new contacts on this Sunday, most likely people who will become firm friends and who are in a good position to offer you some timely support.

28 MONDAY   *Moon Age Day 1   Moon Sign Scorpio*

Social gatherings should be a breeze at the moment. You have exactly what it takes to get on well with the crowd and any shyness that typifies Pisces seems to be taking a holiday for the moment. Don't be in too much of a rush to get a particular job done. It would be best to wait a while and to make sure it is done properly.

29 TUESDAY   *Moon Age Day 2   Moon Sign Scorpio*

One-to-one relationships tend to make you feel warm and secure right now, while more formal or distant ones could present a potential problem of some sort. Although you may struggle with confidence, you should be able to do what it takes to smooth things over, even if you feel you are quaking inside.

30 WEDNESDAY   *Moon Age Day 3   Moon Sign Sagittarius*

Get-togethers with others should now prove to be highly rewarding. It doesn't really matter whether these are related to social events or to work. You will be making a big effort to cut through any red tape and certainly won't take kindly to needless rules and regulations.

31 THURSDAY   *Moon Age Day 4   Moon Sign Sagittarius*

It can benefit you greatly to keep in touch with people who are in the know in any area of life. Your generally affable ways make you popular with most people. Turn this to your advantage for once and call in some assistance. As you move towards the culmination of plans you hatched some time ago, you may make material progress.

November

2019

1 FRIDAY
☿ *Moon Age Day 5   Moon Sign Sagittarius*

At home the advice of a loved one can prove to be very important. You are probably far better off listening today rather than being the one who is handing out the homilies. Routines could be comfortable and you may prefer to settle for second-best than to push yourself.

2 SATURDAY
☿ *Moon Age Day 6   Moon Sign Capricorn*

A discussion could be the cause of some irritation, which is why it might be best not to get too involved today if you can avoid doing so. Stick to what you know and keep to your own little corner if you feel in any way threatened. The planets are supporting you and personal relationships look good.

3 SUNDAY
☿ *Moon Age Day 7   Moon Sign Capricorn*

There are some excellent influences around when it comes to looking and planning ahead. With plenty of positive feedback coming in and a desire to break the bounds of the credible, you can make this a rewarding and stimulating interlude. The opinions of friends vary wildly around now.

4 MONDAY
☿ *Moon Age Day 8   Moon Sign Aquarius*

Emotional relationships and issues between yourself and your partner can seem more trouble than they are worth at first today. If this rings true for you, keep things simple. You haven't really got the time or the inclination to be involved in disputes at work either. Stick to your own corner, at least until nearer the end of the day.

5 TUESDAY ☿ *Moon Age Day 9   Moon Sign Aquarius*

This may prove to be a time of versatility and mental dexterity. Having several interests on the go at the same time would be rewarding and there isn't any doubt about your ability to turn heads in social and romantic situations. Just take care you don't provoke a little unnecessary jealousy in someone else.

6 WEDNESDAY ☿ *Moon Age Day 10   Moon Sign Pisces*

It might be quite easy for others to take exception to your views today but that is hardly your fault. You can't please all of the people all of the time and there's no real point in trying to do so. If you stick to your guns and remain confident, those who are important will soon follow your reasoning.

7 THURSDAY ☿ *Moon Age Day 11   Moon Sign Pisces*

The lunar high arrives and should bring with it one of the more fortunate periods during November. You are especially intuitive now and very resourceful. This is a time during which you really do have to believe in yourself because when it is obvious that you do, everyone else will fall in line.

8 FRIDAY ☿ *Moon Age Day 12   Moon Sign Pisces*

Take advantage of the very promising influences that stand around you now. You are bright, easy-going, adventurous and very good to know. What more could the world ask? Most important of all you must believe in yourself because there is very little that lies beyond your capabilities now.

9 SATURDAY ☿ *Moon Age Day 13   Moon Sign Aries*

Planetary influences now suggest that certain meaningful ambitions are within your reach. Superiors at work may lend you a helping hand and are likely to offer you new incentives and responsibilities. It is up to you to prove that you are equal to the task. This should also be a good time romantically.

10 SUNDAY ☿ *Moon Age Day 14   Moon Sign Aries*

Group work, teamwork and all social matters are inclined to go well for you now. You want to keep life varied and interesting and there is plenty of help around to do so. The chances are that you will do equally well at work or in social situations. You might have to be just a little careful not to give someone the wrong romantic impression, though.

11 MONDAY ☿ *Moon Age Day 15   Moon Sign Taurus*

The opportunities for financial advancement are especially good at the moment. You can afford to chance your arm a little more and you should rely on your intuition to lead you in the right direction. When it comes to your personal life it looks as though you are in for a varied but quite stimulating time.

12 TUESDAY ☿ *Moon Age Day 16   Moon Sign Taurus*

You will most likely prefer to be on the move today and may choose involve yourself in a variety of different interests. All the same, there might be one special goal that is worth pursuing, so keep this close to the forefront of your mind. Chance meetings may have far-reaching implications.

13 WEDNESDAY ☿ *Moon Age Day 17   Moon Sign Taurus*

A varied and interesting day now beckons and any slightly negative trends in your chart seem to be disappearing. You function extremely well in company and can find exactly the right words to influence those around you, particularly at work. The evening should offer a total change of pace.

14 THURSDAY ☿ *Moon Age Day 18   Moon Sign Gemini*

Discussions to do with travel may be the cause of some irritation, especially if others are not on the same wavelength as you are. You might need to be rather more assertive than of late if you don't want to be left at the back of any particular queue. The closer you get to finishing a specific task, the more awkward it might seem to be.

15 FRIDAY ☿ *Moon Age Day 19   Moon Sign Gemini*

This is a time during which you need to think big and to work to the best of your abilities. Even if this is not particularly relevant in the workplace today, you will have the ability to get things sorted out for the days ahead because the positive trends surrounding you now will be around for a few days.

16 SATURDAY ☿ *Moon Age Day 20   Moon Sign Cancer*

Current trends leave you with some new directions to travel, either in a real or a figurative sense. You might not be feeling particularly brave at present but this doesn't show and just about everyone you meet thinks you are the bee's knees. Don't be too quick to step aside in favour of someone else in any situation.

17 SUNDAY ☿ *Moon Age Day 21   Moon Sign Cancer*

A significant intellectual boost makes itself felt around this time. Good conversation is something you really enjoy this weekend and you may also have a stronger influence on the actions of your partner or family members than you might have expected. There are possible new rewards around most corners.

18 MONDAY ☿ *Moon Age Day 22   Moon Sign Leo*

You will be attending to a number of different jobs today but like the juggler you are it is possible to keep all the balls in the air at the same time. Not everyone believes in you right now but the people who matter the most will and that should be enough to see you through one or two potentially sticky moments.

19 TUESDAY ☿ *Moon Age Day 23   Moon Sign Leo*

Trends now centre on home and family, making you less involved in professional or practical matters, at least for one day. You need the reassurance that comes from close partnerships, and Pisceans who are not in a relationship might well be finding one in the not too distant future.

20 WEDNESDAY ☿   *Moon Age Day 24*   *Moon Sign Leo*

When it comes to furthering your ambitions you are clearly second to none, even though you might have to enlist the support of others on the way. Prepare for some unexpected events around this time and you will manage to deal with them relatively easily. A new relationship of some kind could be on the way.

21 THURSDAY   *Moon Age Day 25*   *Moon Sign Virgo*

It is towards your social life that your mind is most likely to turn, and travel arrangements look like being your second best area just at the moment. There's no harm in standing still for a while. All Pisceans need interludes during which they can meditate and plan for the future. This is one of yours.

22 FRIDAY   *Moon Age Day 26*   *Moon Sign Virgo*

A plan of action is likely to fall flat today and for this you can blame the lunar low. You certainly won't be on top form and could feel as if you are walking through treacle, especially where your professional life is concerned. This is nothing but a short interlude and so don't worry too much about it.

23 SATURDAY   *Moon Age Day 27*   *Moon Sign Libra*

There isn't much doubt about your ability to turn on the charm right now and it's worth making the most out of every potential situation now your trends have picked up. There are some jobs in which you seem to take three steps forward and two back but at least you are making some sort of progress.

24 SUNDAY   *Moon Age Day 28*   *Moon Sign Libra*

Close companions may now cause you to think quite deeply about the importance you have placed upon relationships of late. It is possible that you might decide to spend some of your social hours with people you don't see very often. This would be a good day for sending letters or for making a long-distance telephone call.

25 MONDAY   *Moon Age Day 29   Moon Sign Scorpio*

New life may be breathed into situations you thought were over and done with today. It looks very likely that someone will share a confidence with you and you will be expected to keep it. Friends are likely to be particularly demanding of your time and that won't leave quite as many hours as you might have wished for practical matters.

26 TUESDAY   *Moon Age Day 0   Moon Sign Scorpio*

You can make an extremely powerful impression on those further up the tree than you are and will want to do everything you can to be noticed at the moment. There is much to be gained from being in the spotlight, even if to be so goes against the Piscean grain in one way or another. This would be a great time to take a trip.

27 WEDNESDAY   *Moon Age Day 1   Moon Sign Sagittarius*

You might prove to be far too impetuous regarding the decisions you are making today and, if so, should bear in mind that it is better to give things proper consideration. Although you might not feel you have the confidence of family members, in all probability they will back you when it really counts. Don't become drawn into pointless arguments.

28 THURSDAY   *Moon Age Day 2   Moon Sign Sagittarius*

Your intuition will now stand you in good stead, especially if you turn it in the direction of people who are coming new into your life. These might be people who you meet on a professional level or perhaps potential friends for the future. Bear in mind that not everything is what it seems to be.

29 FRIDAY   *Moon Age Day 3   Moon Sign Capricorn*

Avoid being too pushy at the moment because it probably won't get you very far. Instead, display the humility that is part of the basic nature of your zodiac sign and then you will have everyone eating out of your hand. Your confidence grows by the moment, especially if you are doing professional jobs you understand.

30 SATURDAY *Moon Age Day 4   Moon Sign Capricorn*

Self-confidence in professional matters will get you a long way, but you won't get anywhere at all if you fail to show those around you that you know what you are talking about. In social and family situations you are clearly putting everyone ahead of yourself, which isn't unusual for Pisces.

December

2019

1 SUNDAY
Moon Age Day 5   Moon Sign Aquarius

The things that are the most enjoyable now are to be found out there in the wider world. With plenty to play for and more than a modicum of good luck on your side, you can afford to back your hunches a little. People you haven't seen for some time might soon be in touch and some trends indicate that correspondence could prove to be important.

2 MONDAY
Moon Age Day 6   Moon Sign Aquarius

The things you learn from colleagues today can be of supreme importance, so it is very important to pay attention to what is being said. Pisceans who are looking for work or a change of employment could also be in luck around this time. When it comes to out-of-work activities, new interests take your fancy.

3 TUESDAY
Moon Age Day 7   Moon Sign Aquarius

The ideas that others have will not be exactly to your liking now and you are much more likely to think for yourself. Whether or not you can bring important people round to your way of thinking remains to be seen. There are some quite significant changes coming for some Pisceans.

4 WEDNESDAY
Moon Age Day 8   Moon Sign Pisces

Getting into heated debates could be more enjoyable than you might imagine and as the lunar high has come around you are hardly likely to lose. Back your hunches to the hilt and do anything you can to make progress. There isn't too much time before the holidays, so get your shopping skates on.

5 THURSDAY
Moon Age Day 9   Moon Sign Pisces

Trends may offer you a lucky break now and you won't be inclined to look on the negative side of any situation at present. Getting favours from others should prove to be especially easy it seems you are especially popular. In reality, you are always popular but perhaps you realise it more at this time.

6 FRIDAY
Moon Age Day 10   Moon Sign Aries

It is now the practical aspects of life that appeal to you the most. In the main, you will want to do your own thing today and won't take kindly to being bossed around by anyone. The end of a particular phase in your life is not too far away and although it may be accompanied by the odd sigh of nostalgia, the gains outweigh the losses.

7 SATURDAY
Moon Age Day 11   Moon Sign Aries

You will enjoy being on the move as much as possible but don't allow distractions to get in the way of real financial success. Dragging yourself back to practicalities might not seem all that inspiring but could prove to be quite important all the same. It is also a good time to get your Christmas head on.

8 SUNDAY
Moon Age Day 12   Moon Sign Aries

Don't dither or hang back when it comes to making major decisions. The more ambitious you are, the greater is your potential for success. Results you have been seeking for some time will be closer than you think and you have tremendous potential for doing just the right thing when it matters the most.

9 MONDAY
Moon Age Day 13   Moon Sign Taurus

The planetary emphasis falls on finances, which is probably not surprising at this expensive time of the year. You are quite canny at the moment and know full well how to get value for money. Keep looking because there could be one or two things available for Christmas that you get at rock bottom prices.

10 TUESDAY   *Moon Age Day 14   Moon Sign Taurus*

A possible mistake you might make today is to take on too many diverse interests. You would be much better off concentrating on one thing at a time and avoiding unnecessary mistakes. Methodical tasks lead to gain but there will still be plenty of time in which to enjoy yourself.

11 WEDNESDAY   *Moon Age Day 15   Moon Sign Gemini*

A sense of variety and freedom is both important and appealing to Pisceans at this time. Don't be a stick-in-the-mud. Although this might not be exactly the season for outdoor activities, you might find the call of the wild appealing. Later in the day, you might choose to spend at least some time alone.

12 THURSDAY   *Moon Age Day 16   Moon Sign Gemini*

Although there might be a few letdowns to contend with today, in the main the day ought to be fairly smooth running. You can rely pretty much on the good offices of friends and should also discover something to your advantage at work. It's really a case of keeping your eyes open.

13 FRIDAY   *Moon Age Day 17   Moon Sign Cancer*

It is likely that you will get what you expect or perhaps hope for from the responses of loved ones right now. Domestic matters are likely to be on your mind but that won't prevent you from making generally good progress in practical matters too. Keep an eye open for the chance of a little adventure that could be on the way.

14 SATURDAY   *Moon Age Day 18   Moon Sign Cancer*

This ought to be a very favourable day for all practical matters but don't put off current projects until it's too late to do them. You need to be flexible at the moment and to respond to situations as and when necessary. Romance could be coming your way later and you should have some plans that make this weekend go well.

15 SUNDAY
Moon Age Day 19   Moon Sign Cancer

There is likely to be someone around who is more than willing to put themselves out on your behalf and their opinions are worth a lot. Attitude is all-important when you are facing issues over which you have little experience, together with a willingness to be extra flexible.

16 MONDAY
Moon Age Day 20   Moon Sign Leo

It would be all too easy today to get caught up in disagreements regarding the various rights and wrongs of situations. Ask yourself if anything will be changed as a result of these differences of opinion. Better by far to maintain your cheerful attitude and to refuse to be drawn into trouble.

17 TUESDAY
Moon Age Day 21   Moon Sign Leo

It may have slipped your mind somewhat across the last week but Christmas is just around the corner. In amongst what is likely to be a very busy life, you need to get those festive details sorted out. This year may be unusual for you in that it is lacking the deeply nostalgic frame of mind that Pisces is often in at this time.

18 WEDNESDAY
Moon Age Day 22   Moon Sign Virgo

Some of the things that are happening around you at present seem less fulfilling than you would like. You need to broaden your horizons somewhat and should not be intimidated by little setbacks. The lunar low doesn't really help the situation but whether or not you enjoy what today has on offer seems to be up to you.

19 THURSDAY
Moon Age Day 23   Moon Sign Virgo

There is no sense in arguing about particular incidents if that means upsetting those around you. Medium and longer-term issues should be put on hold, so that you can give most of your attention to enjoying what your social life has to offer. Younger people figure most in your thinking today.

20 FRIDAY
Moon Age Day 24   Moon Sign Libra

Social matters look particularly favourable and this ought to be a very happy sort of Friday, unless of course you have to work hard. Professional trends are not quite so well-starred now, and it could be that too much is being demanded of you. If you can spend time with family and friends, it is with them that you find the most fun.

21 SATURDAY
Moon Age Day 25   Moon Sign Libra

It is what rather than who you know that helps you to get ahead now. Rely on your own knowledge, together with a big helping of intuition, in order to make the right moves. It doesn't matter what others tell you because in the end you want to approach life in your own way. Be diplomatic but plough your own furrow.

22 SUNDAY
Moon Age Day 26   Moon Sign Scorpio

The things that are happening in your social life now become more important and more rewarding. It could be that you have decided that to make any serious ground professionally, with Christmas so close, is something of a waste of time. Friends have suggestions to make that you might find hard to refuse.

23 MONDAY
Moon Age Day 27   Moon Sign Scorpio

Your social life ought to be bringing out the best in you, but you are likely to be just a little introspective and not quite as inclined to let your hair down as will be the case by tomorrow. You might decide to settle for a quiet evening, perhaps with your partner or the family, but that can bring its own form of joy.

24 TUESDAY
Moon Age Day 28   Moon Sign Sagittarius

Although you may feel the need to stay indoors and to soak up the Christmas spirit, you are still likely to have a particularly good and enjoyable day. Travel is most likely to come later in the holidays. For the moment, you should be at home feeling warm, secure and surrounded by love.

25 WEDNESDAY *Moon Age Day 29   Moon Sign Sagittarius*

You are on a high this Christmas Day and will be sought out by others because of your attractive personality and natural warmth. There are likely to be few frustrations in your life at this time and you can also expect to be lucky. Don't worry about keeping a sense of proportion. You don't need one today.

26 THURSDAY *Moon Age Day 0   Moon Sign Capricorn*

This Boxing Day is a time for enjoying the company of others for its own sake. You appear to have no agenda whatsoever today – a concept that is more understandable to Pisces than to any other zodiac sign. Just enjoy being who you are, doing what you're doing for now. That will be more than enough for you.

27 FRIDAY *Moon Age Day 1   Moon Sign Capricorn*

Your friendly approach to others continues to make you attractive to the people around you. It doesn't matter who you mix with at this time because you are very adaptable. Attitude is very important when you are facing new situations, which could easily be the case under present trends. Family members might be slightly overbearing, though.

28 SATURDAY *Moon Age Day 2   Moon Sign Capricorn*

The ordinary daily comings and goings of life have a particular appeal for you now, and it is likely that you are slightly tired of having a good time. You need a sense of normality in your life so will happily tackle all manner of domestic chores with great cheerfulness. Don't count too much on people you either don't know or have only recently met.

29 SUNDAY *Moon Age Day 3   Moon Sign Aquarius*

As you grow more and more confident, so you are less intimidated by finding yourself in the limelight. It is true that others will be making a fuss of you at the moment and you are likely to make the most of it. Today is also very good for all aspects of romance and one-to-one encounters.

30 MONDAY
Moon Age Day 4   Moon Sign Aquarius

Work undertaken as part of a team is your most favoured area under present planetary trends, though you clearly know how to enjoy yourself too, and social possibilities are the best for today. Don't worry about making careful arrangements because it is likely to be the sudden and last minute gatherings and functions that are the most exciting.

31 TUESDAY
Moon Age Day 5   Moon Sign Pisces

Personal and family life seems to be your most rewarding area for the last day of the year. You will probably be taking a trip down memory lane but there is nothing strange about this for Pisces, particularly at this time of year. Stand by for plenty of fun brought about by the lunar high tonight.

RISING SIGNS FOR PISCES

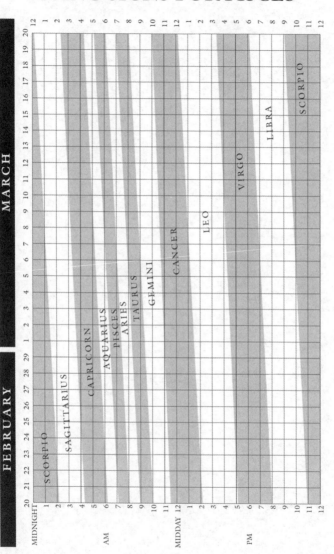

THE ZODIAC, PLANETS AND CORRESPONDENCES

The Earth revolves around the Sun once every calendar year, so when viewed from Earth the Sun appears in a different part of the sky as the year progresses. In astrology, these parts of the sky are divided into the signs of the zodiac and this means that the signs are organised in a circle. The circle begins with Aries and ends with Pisces.

Taking the zodiac sign as a starting point, astrologers then work with all the positions of planets, stars and many other factors to calculate horoscopes and birth charts and tell us what the stars have in store for us.

The table below shows the planets and Elements for each of the signs of the zodiac. Each sign belongs to one of the four Elements: Fire, Air, Earth or Water. Fire signs are creative and enthusiastic; Air signs are mentally active and thoughtful; Earth signs are constructive and practical; Water signs are emotional and have strong feelings.

It also shows the metals and gemstones associated with, or corresponding with, each sign. The correspondence is made when a metal or stone possesses properties that are held in common with a particular sign of the zodiac.

Finally, the table shows the opposite of each star sign – this is the opposite sign in the astrological circle.

Placed	Sign	Symbol	Element	Planet	Metal	Stone	Opposite
1	Aries	Ram	Fire	Mars	Iron	Bloodstone	Libra
2	Taurus	Bull	Earth	Venus	Copper	Sapphire	Scorpio
3	Gemini	Twins	Air	Mercury	Mercury	Tiger's Eye	Sagittarius
4	Cancer	Crab	Water	Moon	Silver	Pearl	Capricorn
5	Leo	Lion	Fire	Sun	Gold	Ruby	Aquarius
6	Virgo	Maiden	Earth	Mercury	Mercury	Sardonyx	Pisces
7	Libra	Scales	Air	Venus	Copper	Sapphire	Aries
8	Scorpio	Scorpion	Water	Pluto	Plutonium	Jasper	Taurus
9	Sagittarius	Archer	Fire	Jupiter	Tin	Topaz	Gemini
10	Capricorn	Goat	Earth	Saturn	Lead	Black Onyx	Cancer
11	Aquarius	Waterbearer	Air	Uranus	Uranium	Amethyst	Leo
12	Pisces	Fishes	Water	Neptune	Tin	Moonstone	Virgo